'Cornwall'
Transition from Steam

PASSENGERS ARE
REQUESTED TO CROSS
THE LINE BY MEANS
OF THE BRIDGE

9
CAR

6828

The R C Riley Archive: Vol 6
Compiled by Jeremy Clements

The
· Transport ·
Treasury

© Images and design: The Transport Treasury 2021. Text Jeremy Clements.

ISBN 978-1-913251-17-8

First published in 2021 by Transport Treasury Publishing Ltd., 16 Highworth Close, High Wycombe, HP13 7PJ

www.ttpublishing.co.uk

Printed in the UK by Henry Ling Limited at the Dorset Press, Dorchester. DT1 1HD

Front Cover: The 4-6-0 Counties were a popular type for heavier trains in Cornwall with plenty of power and good hill-climbing ability. On 9 July 1955, No. 1018 *County of Leicester* was leading 2-6-0 Class 43xx No. 6305 on the climb to the 565-yard long Treverrin Tunnel on what must have been a heavily loaded Down train. The leading coaches reflect a mixed composition typical of the period, first a Collett Diagram D118 Brake Third of 1934/ 5, then a Hawksworth coach (probably an All Third) and then a BR Mark 1 All Third. The train is crossing Milltown viaduct, originally a Class A 7-pier timber structure it had been 501' long with a maximum height above the valley floor of 75' and was replaced on the Up side with this all-stone version in 1896. The "double-header" is about to pass an Up service drifting down the bank in the care of an unidentified County. *RCR6361*

Frontispiece: The Granges were ideally suited for a variety of mixed traffic duties, including even working the "Cornish Riviera" between Plymouth and Penzance. On 9 July 1961, No. 6828 *Trellech Grange* (a resident of Truro from November 1958 until October 1961) was at Liskeard and engaged on duties at the other end of the spectrum. Carrying the headcode for pick-up or branch goods, this smartly turned-out engine was drawing out on to the Down main line from the line that looped around to connect with the sharply curved 1 in 40 gradient that descended into the Looe Valley at Coombe Junction. The 4-6-0 must have called to collect or leave wagons related to traffic that would have been worked over the branch by a 45xx prairie. The locomotive's condition suggests that it is not long out of the works and its only blemish seems to be a missing shed code plate. *RCR16057*

Opposite: It appears occasionally to the side in his photographs, so here is a full view of Dick Riley's cherished chariot, his Morris Minor Tourer. This car was used over many years as an essential tool in his photographic odyssey. Train services in Cornwall were not frequent so the gathering of 700+ images at diverse locations would have been impossible without this essential equipment. The pedigree of the decrepit 7-plank open wagon has defied identification. *RCR5216*

Rear Cover: Steam was still being used on branch freight services after passenger duties had been dieselised as in the case of small prairie No. 5573 on 14 July 1961 at Bodmin with the sub-shed in the background. The china clay wagon seems to have been a private owner vehicle in an earlier life, given its number P387418. Normally a 5-plank wagon would be restricted to an 8 or 10 ton load but the designated 12 ton capacity reflects the greater density of clay and the vehicle's sound condition. The number is in the P290351-391500 series which were being distributed in blocks of 50 when in 1957 British Railways abandoned the herculean task of rationalising the identities of its ex-PO wagons. Records of which numbers had been allocated and to whom apparently no longer exist for this series. *RCR16088*

Contents

Introduction

The Railway Mania had long passed by the time the concept of a line to traverse the length of the Cornish peninsular had evolved from pipe dream into a substantive challenge for engineer and investor. Commercial prospects were unimpressive. The county was physically remote, underpopulated and to a significant extent impoverished with an economy reliant on agriculture, fishing and extraction of mineral wealth. The first two sustained the local population while the transport needs of the third were served by canals and primitive tramways that followed a broadly north-south axis, taking advantage of the contours to connect mines and quarries with seaports.

Broad Gauge penetration of Devon had revealed the civil engineering challenges presented by the West Country. Lacking the severity of Dartmoor's southern shoulders, Cornwall's terrain was less extreme but no less difficult, punctuated by a succession of valleys. The difficult topography and scarce investment capital made a saw-tooth gradient profile and many twists and turns unavoidable. However, the single most demanding feature lay in the succession of valleys that drained the land. No other line in Britain confronted so many over so short a distance, and the manner in which they were tackled was an act of genius typical of their creator.

Brunel's timber viaducts were a brilliant compromise in the face of demands to complete the operating railway, to surmount the physical constraints, and to overcome shortage of capital. Each location necessitated a uniquely tailored solution and, indeed, two different structural designs were adopted in the three water crossings installed by the Cornwall Railway even before it reached Cornwall (at Stonehouse Pool, Keyham and Weston Mill).

The challenges beyond Plymouth endowed the route with a unique and enduring character. Exploitation of favourable contours partially met the need but a series of short, sharp ups and downs were unavoidable. Even then, westbound trains faced two climbs much in the mould of Dainton and Rattery/ Hemerdon. From a mile west of Par, there was a continuous climb of varying steepness over five miles through St Austell to just short of Burngullow while beyond Truro there was almost three miles at 1 in 80 before reaching Chacewater. High speeds to help circumvent these obstacles were frustrated by the curvaceous alignment. Locomotive crews thus faced conditions of a character far removed from, for example, another of Brunel's creations, the 'finest work in England' through the Thames Valley.

In the years of Dick Riley's visits, Cornwall remained remote through geography and by virtue of the River Tamar. This would change with completion of the long-awaited road crossing, which coincided with the end of steam in the west. His collection surveys an earlier time when the railway served the community in an intensely localised sense. For the indigenous population it was an important conduit of communication, trade and personal movement. The images impart an impression of a world where railway personnel knew well not only their colleagues but also a sizeable proportion of the local population they served.

The steam population was also of localised character. It was familiarly Great Western but subtly different in its composition. Fewer classes were used and many individual locomotives were long-term residents. It seems probable that some rarely ventured as far east as Newton Abbot, and then only for attention in the old South Devon Railway's works. The profile of shed allocations imparts a sense of simplicity and of focus on locomotives best suited to the work in hand. Hopefully, the views that follow capture the flavour of an interesting and individualistic corner of the (Great) Western Region's empire.
.

--- o O o ---

Following the appearance of *Western Region Non-Passenger Trains* (Transport Treasury Publishing 2020), a reader challenged how it was possible to be so definitive about train composition with long rakes of vehicles disappearing into the distance. One of the many pleasures in preparing this and the previous two works has been the opportunity to help rectify a shortcoming apparent with photographs in books and contemporary periodicals, as exemplified with a published photograph of an 0-4-2T Class 14xx at Shrewsbury in the 1950s. The caption merely identified the class, the engine number (already prominently visible on the smokebox door) and the station. A letter to the magazine editor followed, pointing out that the train had been ignored despite it consisting of an interesting pair of 70' auto trailers, one of which was a Steam Rail Motor conversion. It was proposed that captions should include details about the duty depicted, the rolling stock, plus the static and mobile "railway furniture", so much of which has been sanitised from the modern system. The editor's courteous response advised that the suggested information was not readily to hand. This was simply not the case then, and is even less so now.

As the collection has been scanned, the compiler enjoys an advantage in being able to magnify images. Coupled with their excellence this process yields a mass of detail not otherwise visible, enabling an attempt at an expanded picture in words. Filling the gaps is detective work that relies on the reference library, as detailed in the Bibliography. Atlases, route maps and station diagrams are invaluable in confirming locations and direction of travel. Rolling stock often is the most time-consuming but distinctive body profiles, counting doors and measuring window spacings all help to isolate a vehicle's vintage and type. Many GWR passenger trains were a glorious mixture but there were consistencies as with catering vehicles in the centre of a set, and often older than their companions. Informative publications on diagram numbers, train reporting numbers for main line passenger services and goods trains' headlamp codes all help to dissect and re-assemble the jigsaw.

Despite all this published information and regardless of how thorough is the desk research, local knowledge can overrule these endeavours. For example, a photograph of a breakdown train in *Western Region Non-Passenger Trains* was reported as at Langford Bridge on the Westbury-Salisbury line, following exhaustive research. However, Nicolas Trudgian marshalled his comprehensive local

knowledge to advise that the location was actually on the lower stretches of Dainton East.

These studies concern events of sixty years and more ago. As Anno Domini takes its toll upon the memory, the imperative of accuracy is not always easily satisfied. Contributions and corrections are welcome in recording the fine work of a gifted photographer, and the key features and minutiae of a great institution. It would have been rash not to allow Cornishman Nicolas to review this work. His assistance is gratefully acknowledged but all errors and omissions still remain the sole responsibility of the undersigned.

Jeremy Clements
Co Meath
November 2020

Bibliography

AG Atkins, W Beard, R Tourret	GWR Goods Wagons	OPC 2013
John Binding	Brunel's Cornish Viaducts	Pendragon Publishing/ HMRS 1993
Jeremy Clements	The GWR Exposed	OPC 2015
RA Cooke	Atlas of the GWR as at 1947	Wild Swan Publications 1988
RA Cooke	Track Layout Diagrams of the GWR & BR (WR) Sections 10 & 11	Lightmoor Press 2020
Michael Harris	Great Western Coaches from 1890	David & Charles 1985
Hugh Longworth	British Railways Pre-Nationalisation Coaching Stock Vol 1	OPC 2018
E Lyons	An Historical Survey of Great Western Engine Sheds 1947	OPC 1972
Railway Correspondence & Travel Society	The Locomotives of the Great Western Railway	1951 et seq
Ian Sixsmith	The 2-8-0T Tank Papers	Irwell Press 2017
Xpress Publishing	The Xpress Locomotive Register, Volume 4	Xpress Publishing, Undated

Previously a long term resident at Weymouth, by 21 June 1962 Collett dockyard 0-6-0PT No. 1368 was busy shunting in Southern territory at Wadebridge. *RCR16571*

Chapter 1

Viaduct

The railway that traversed the Duchy was uniquely defined by river and valley crossings. Over the 80 miles between Plymouth and Penzance, there were 36 such features on the main line of the Cornwall Railway as far as Truro and ten more on the West Cornwall Railway from Penwithers Junction. There were another eight on the 9-mile branch of the CR from Penwithers to Falmouth. Over five miles of railway were borne by these structures of which all but two made substantial use of timber, a material in which their designer was well versed.

The basic form comprised masonry foundations and piers that supported fans of timber beams on which was laid horizontal decking. This was a stroke of genius typical of IK Brunel's enormous talent. Otherwise, traditional stone-arched viaducts would have been beyond the new railway's financial resources. Construction and assembly was also achieved faster, making his invention crucial for the viability of the of the whole project.

Brunel surveyed the route in the early 1850s but he delegated construction of the railway to his Chief Assistant, RP Brereton. Another assistant, W Bell, who as a young man worked on the project, would later emerge as a pre-eminent authority on the theory of structures. A further protégé, HS Bush, was Engineer for the Cornwall Railway until his death in 1868. His successor, PJ Margary, yet another of Brunel's young assistants, played the dominant role in the later stages of the timber viaduct story until retirement in 1891 by which time replacement was well under way. None remained on the main line after 1908; those on the Falmouth branch were removed between 1923 and 1934.

Brunel had calculated annual maintenance costs at around £10,000 (then a substantial sum) and experience would prove this to be an under-estimate.

Early problems were due to sub-standard masonry work by some subcontractors, necessitating demolition and re-start in some cases; the well-known but troubled Moorswater viaduct near Liskeard was a prominent example. The timber sections were exclusively fashioned from long-lasting yellow pine which was shipped to Lostwithiel where it was cut to pre-determined sizes and then preserved by either highly toxic mercury chloride or less virulent zinc chloride. The project consumed almost one million cubic feet of pine and, in the later stages, varying texture caused difficulties as good quality timber became increasingly hard to find.

Margary classified the viaducts A to E, depending upon their principle design features. Category A was the most common and the most spectacular, of which there were 27. With this type, stone piers rose to about 35' below track level, providing the base for three fans of timber struts that radiated at angles between 55 and 125 degrees to the horizontal to support beams that formed the viaduct platform. On average, the vertical centres of the piers were 65 feet apart. The timber beams were seated in and connected to each other through cast iron chairs, and where under tension they were bound by wrought iron tie rods. Despite the preservatives and yellow pine's longevity, decay was unavoidable where moisture collected e.g. cast iron chair seatings, bolt holes, and the horizontal decking. An intensive maintenance regime by skilled (and brave) crews was necessary; all individual timber components could be replaced without interrupting services, except for imposition of temporary speed restrictions.

In 1871, the 435' long viaduct at Probus was the first to be replaced, in this case by an embankment. Other methods were route deviation or construction of new viaducts using stone or steel girders. Parts of

some Class A viaducts remained in use where the original piers formed bases for brick or stone upward extensions to support spans assembled using steel girders as at Liskeard. Elsewhere (e.g. Moorswater and Cavedras in Truro), the route was realigned for a new all stone construction, leaving the original piers in place alongside. That at St. Austell was more complex as most of the replacement was on a new alignment but limitations at the eastern end enforced use of the old structure.

Despite their ingenious design and distinctive appearance, the timber viaducts were unpopular with passengers. At a time when trains were the fastest form of travel and powered flight lay in an unimaginable future, crossing a valley at speed and at a great height was terrifying for some. Fear was accentuated by creaking and groaning of the timbers induced by the train's passage, and by the tendency

of the spans to flex and move under load. Even so, no passengers suffered physical injury from these experiences. The same cannot be said of construction and maintenance crews who worked with poisonous materials at dizzying heights and with minimal safety measures.

The viaducts served a vital purpose but their limitations were evident with the last in service, Collegewood (Class A, MP 309½, 14 piers, height 100', length 954') which was the most southerly on the Falmouth branch. In its closing years it could accept a locomotive no heavier than a Class 45xx prairie. A replacement stone structure was completed in 1934; the original piers remain alongside in silent salute to a brilliant idea.

--- o O o ---

Left and Right: Welcome to Cornwall! Following departure from the Cornwall Railway's eastern terminus at Plymouth Millbay, the fourth water crossing as different from the others and definitely not of timber construction, excluding the baulk road trackwork laid on its decking. Indeed, this crossing was different from any other bridge or viaduct in Britain, although some of the radical construction principles had been successfully tried out in 1852 with the unusual Chepstow Bridge over the River Wye on the South Wales Railway. The River Tamar was a major barrier that largely isolated south-eastern Cornwall from Plymouth before the coming of the railway. The only other means of access were by ferries or by the lowest road bridge at Gunnislake, about 10 miles north of Plymouth as the crow flies. Brunel built his bridge at the only viable location but the challenge was compounded by the necessity for curved approaches on both sides, by the depth of the water, and by the Admiralty's requirement for sufficient headroom to allow passage of sailing vessels.

Saltash station stands on a curve as the main line turns southwards to run down the western bank of the Tamar. This was a good vantage point from which to view the bridge as the station could hardly have been

closer. On 13 July 1956, an auto train had left Devon and was about to enter the Duchy. This photograph was taken from the station and the second shows the same train arriving at the Down platform. Having left the single track section, the fireman of 0-6-0PT No. 6414 (Laira), one of five members of Class 64xx allocated to Laira that summer, has just hung the token on the "cow's horn" as the train draws to a halt.

The auto coach cannot be firmly identified as the number *appears* to be W61W which if correct would place it in 70' Diagram L. Alternatively it could be a Diagram P vehicle which had an identical body style but different seating arrangements. The time is not recorded but as the train comprises a single coach this must be an off-peak service from North Road. It was more normal for workings to consist of four auto coaches with a Class 64xx sandwiched in the middle. Single coach trains did work on to St. Germans and Menheniot but the destination board at the extreme left suggests that this service would terminate at Saltash. The top of the starting signal (down platform to single line) is missing on the negative. *RCR7617, 7618*

Opposite: A Hall 4-6-0 was crossing the Royal Albert Bridge on 3 September 1954 with a Down passenger train. The best way to view the bridge during the 1950s was from the deck of the Saltash ferry as seen below the western span. *RCR5420*

Above: On 28 August 1961, 0-6-0PT No. 6400 (Laira) with an auto train was standing at Saltash station's Down platform while taking water. Built in September 1954 to Diagram A34, No W244W was the last purpose-built auto coach to enter service; its career was short with withdrawal taking place in August 1966. In another work in this series, this coach was found doing duty on the Ashburton branch. *RCR16193*

Right: On the same day, a Plymouth-bound two-car diesel multiple unit was leaving Saltash. The railway crossing is overshadowed by the taller, much-needed road bridge which was then almost complete. Publicly opened for road traffic two months after this photograph was taken, the new construction greatly detracted from the spectacular impact of Brunel's masterpiece. However, it is some compensation that the southern walkway of the modern bridge (rebuilt and widened between 1998 and 2001) allows study of the Royal Albert Bridge's unique structure at comparatively close quarters. This view reminds one that the curved approach railway viaducts on both sides of the Tamar were also impressive pieces of civil engineering in their own right. *RCR16194*

Opposite: Moorswater was probably the most spectacular of Brunel's timber viaducts, on account of its 147-foot height, 954-foot length, and the supporting fourteen buttressed piers. It was built (as was its eight-arch all stone replacement alongside to the north) on a gradual curve which is not apparent from the many side photographs of the structure that have been published. As a timber viaduct, it had a problematic history in contrast to the nearby St. Pinnock and Liskeard viaducts which were of similar size and proportions. Records are incomplete but the main cause appears to have been poor workmanship in building the stone piers. Two collapsed during construction in 1855 leading Brunel to suspend work.

As a timber structure it was in service for only 22 years, and its all-stone 8-arch replacement bearing a single broad gauge line was commissioned in 1881. This was widened to accommodate two standard gauge lines in 1893, in which impressive form the viaduct stands today. Doubts about the adequacy of the original masonry were reinforced by the judgement that some of the original piers were unsafe to remain as free-standing structures. From the Plymouth end, six complete piers remain (Nos 3, 4, 9 to 12); Nos 6 to 8 and 11 exist only as stumps; Nos 2 and 5 have been reduced to ground level; and Nos 1 and 14 survive in situ, set in the valley sides.

On 18 July 1960, Dick Riley photographed Moorswater from the south side, showing a Hall crossing with a Down mixed freight train. His next study was taken from the north where No. 4552 (St. Blazey) was busily engaged in freight shunting. The picturesque Moorswater sub-shed is behind the camera to the right. The platform of the long defunct station was buried under the foliage to the left, beside the loop line. *RCR15100, 15108*

Above: This view of Moorswater shed and adjacent sidings, including the remaining stub of the Liskeard & Caradon Railway that served as a head shunt, was taken from a train crossing the viaduct on 2 May 1961. Crossing the valley at such a height would have been understandably frightening when the railway opened. *RCR15703*

Above: The replacement Moorswater viaduct was surmounted by a cast iron balustrade that seemed rather out of place as a stone parapet would surely have been more in keeping with the remainder of the structure. To the right in the valley stand the complete masonry sections of piers Nos. 3 and 4 of the first viaduct, both about 100' tall. Typically with this viaduct type, the top of the pier which provides the base for the timber support fans was about 35' below rail level. The cross-section of the main timber beams of the support fans was one foot x two feet. No 2 pier was reduced to ground level as being unsafe when the new stone viaduct was commissioned while No 1 pier is buried in the trees on the valley side.

The view from this angle allows appreciation of the masonry part of Brunel's structure. The Gothic arches reveal an artistic aspect to the design while the masonry buttresses give a perhaps misleading impression of immense strength. Before the viaduct was brought into service, clusters of enormous vertical timber supports were inserted into all four corners of the buttresses and thick horizontal timber tie beams joined the piers from one end of the viaduct to the other. This arrangement was unique to Moorswater, reinforcing the suspicion that the masonry piers (erected by contractors) were not to the standard that Brunel, always a busy man but by then in declining health, would have expected. The piers were erected without scaffolding which in part explains the high incidence of death and injury among construction workers. Routine replacement of defective timbers was an equally hazardous activity.

On 9 July 1961, No 6860 *Aberporth Grange* was working Up light engine (i.e. with a single Toad attached) towards Liskeard. This engine led a nomadic life between several motive power depots. It had been transferred from Taunton to Laira on 16 June and would be on the move again to Bristol St. Philips Marsh on 19 May 1962. It was withdrawn from Cardiff East Dock in February 1965. *RCR16061*

Opposite top: Moorswater viaduct from yet another angle on Friday 20 August 1954 and judging by the shadows, it is early evening. This ten-coach train is an empty stock working, probably from Plymouth Millbay, bound for Newquay, hauled by St. Blazey's 2-8-0T No. 4247. This locomotive luckily survived into preservation and at the time of writing resides "at home" in the Duchy. On magnification, it is clear that the rake is entirely of GWR provenance, of varying vintages. Frustratingly the distance is too great to identify the diagrams of specific vehicles but the train typifies the mixed composition that would be gathered together for summer Saturday "extra" passenger services. *RCR5341*)

Opposite bottom: Moorswater again on 5 July 1955. The locomotive is recorded as a 59xx series Hall Class and the train would appear to be an inter-regional working consisting of three Hawksworth coaches (Brake Third Diagram D131 or D133, followed by two All Thirds Diagram C82 or C84), a pre-war large-windowed Composite, an unidentified catering vehicle (kitchen section leading), a pre-war Composite (Diagram E158 or E160), a Hawksworth Brake Third, and then two "fillers". The first is an earlier Collett All Third (possibly Diagram C54) and then what looks like an LMS Period II coach. *RCR5762*

Laira's No. 1023 *County of Oxford* was crossing Liskeard viaduct on 10 July 1955 with a Down passenger service that consisted of a typically mixed rake of coaches. The leading vehicle is an early Collett Brake Third followed by a 70' 10-compartment All Third, and then a Diagram E162 Composite. The broad carmine panel below the cant rail and the ducket at the far end betrays the LMS origins of the fourth coach. The seventh carries a roof destination board like the first three and might just be a Toplight. The mixed composition suggests this is an inter-regional working from Birmingham or further north.

This Category A viaduct was completed in 1858, officially located at milepost 264½, with a maximum height of 150' and a length of 720'. As with others in the Liskeard area, difficulties were encountered during construction which was suspended in 1855-6, due to problems with poor work by subcontractors. Background information is apparently lost but remedial work was sufficiently sound for the piers to be extended higher when the timber spans were replaced with lattice steel girders in 1894, and also to support the doubling of the track two years later. The timber spans thus had an operating career of 36 years; corrosion forced replacement of several of the steel girders in 1929 yielding a career of 35 years. The original stone base piers can be clearly seen with the more modern brickwork above. *RCR6390*

On 10 July 1955, large prairie No. 5148 was leading a Down Class H through freight across Liskeard viaduct. The load is around 20 wagons, rounded-off by a Toad with (correctly) the veranda leading – hardly demanding for motive power of this calibre. The mixed composition typifies the variety found in goods trains in those days. This locomotive was a long-term resident of Laira from where it was withdrawn in December 1959.

The prairie is nicely framed by a pair of signals which reveal intricate details of railway equipment that relate to the immediate environment. The Down signal which is "off" is mounted on a wooden post and a "blind" is attached to the operating spindle which blanked out the tell-tale lamp at the rear of the signal lamp when the signal was in this position. This provided visual confirmation to the signalman that the board had moved when its position could not otherwise be seen from the box, for example at night. In this case, the signal box was on the Down side at the end of the platform, and approximately 100 yards behind the camera which meant that the signal was in clear view. In situations where the signal could not be seen from the box, mechanical or electrical repeating equipment was installed whereby the position of the arm appeared on a repeater mounted on the block shelf above the levers.

Turning to the Up bracket signal, the photograph was taken from a position between two short sidings (taken out of use in 1981) that trailed into the main line just short of Liskeard's Down platform. They replaced a turntable removed in 1909 and small engine shed removed in 1918, and were the station's only Down side refuge sidings. Shunting movements within the station limits were confined by the nature of the site, there being no room for expansion at the Plymouth end because of the viaduct. Liskeard's goods shed and yard was at the far (western) end of the station on the Up side. A further complication was provided by the connecting line to the Liskeard and Looe Extension Railway which crossed the Up line and trailed into the Down immediately in front of the signal box. Thus the locomotive of a pick-up goods needing to engage in shunting had to leave its train on either of the main line tracks and use the other for any run-round movements by way of trailing crossovers. There were two, the eastern of which is just in front of the prairie while the other was at the other end of the station, beyond the entrance to the goods shed and yard which trailed into the Up main. To maximise space at the eastern end, the crossover and the Up starting signal is placed as close as possible to the end of the viaduct with the far end of the trailing crossover alongside.

The starting signal protected the next main line section but use of the crossover during shunting required a movement against it while "on". Accordingly, the small "shunt ahead" arm mounted on the main signal post was there to permit this movement. The locomotive could pass the signal to clear the crossover but would have to wait for the ground signal to come off to allow reversal back onto the Down. The ground signal, as revealed in another photograph taken the same day, was located in the six foot between the Up and Down lines (hidden by the prairie in this view). These small-arm signals mounted on posts had a variety of uses where local movements at slow speeds against a main board were necessary. At stations where additional vehicles had to be shunted on to, or removed from, the rear of a train standing in section, they were termed "calling on" signals and at one time were denoted by "CO" in white on the red of the board.

Earlier practice seems to have favoured the mounting of SA/ CO signals below the main board on the same post, but often it was separated by means of a bracket. Here the main arm is mounted on the short post, known as the "doll". Use of a bracket might have been for advance sighting purposes; at this location the line of route is almost straight but there is a very gentle left-hand curve through the station and its buildings might otherwise have been a visual impediment. Normally a bracket signal of this type would have the characteristic finial on the doll and a plain cap to the main post but here the engineers have decided that the main post also deserves that special decoration which sets GWR signals apart from the rest. *RCR6393*

It might be hard to believe that anyone in the civil engineering world could do something better than, or in advance of, Brunel but this sturdy all-stone valley crossing was completed in 1844, well before construction of the Cornwall Railway commenced. This was the work of Joseph Austen who in 1813 had inherited the substantial estates of the Treffry family, following the death of his mother's brother. Austen was an energetic visionary who employed his inheritance in extraction of the mineral wealth north of Par, and who recognised that the Luxulyan Valley provided a natural route to connect mid-Cornwall with the coast. Austen changed his surname to Treffry in 1838 by which time he was well embarked upon a considerable investment programme. His efforts were typical of the Victorian philanthropy exercised by several wealthy individuals that resulted in extensive infrastructural investment, much of which still serves the public good in modern Britain.

Treffry developed mines in the hills, built a new artificial harbour at Par which was commissioned in 1829, and created transport links by way of canal up the Luxulyan Valley plus industrial tramways to bring the extracted ore to the sea for onward shipment. He also reinvigorated the defunct port of Newquay and developed mines on Goss Moor to the north.

The canal penetrated the Luxulyan Valley as far as Ponts Mill and from there an inclined plane railway connected with Fowey Consols mine on Penpillick Hill. To supply the mine with water, Treffry installed a leat along the west side of the valley. Work started on a tramway up the valley but this was soon judged inadequate. It was abandoned in favour of a more ambitious venture that included an inclined plane at Carmears from the canal basin to the top of the valley and then a level section through Luxulyan to a terminus near Mollinis. This route required a high level crossing of the valley through which the River Par runs, which took the form of a stone arch viaduct built entirely of material taken from local quarries.

Although no longer in use, the viaduct, which was completed in 1844, is 89 feet high and comprises nine 40-feet span stone arches. At time of completion it was the most advanced structure in Cornwall. Apart from its height and length, it was also impressive in meeting a dual purpose by carrying Treffry's tramway and by serving as an aqueduct to supply yet more water to Fowey Consols mine. This latter feature emphasised the quality of the construction as the water had to flow at the right pace and in the right volume. Further down the valley, this water flow drove a wheel which in turn powered the tramway's inclined plane at Carmears, as well as a number of other industrial activities in the area.

Treffry died in 1850 by which time his empire was in financial difficulties, a sad close to a saga of endeavour and achievement that had improved the lot of many Cornishmen. Operations continued until 1872 when a consortium of London investors commenced rebuilding and extending the tramway system to tap into ironstone deposits in the Newquay area. Originally designed for operation by horses, the system was up-graded for working by steam, becoming part of the new Cornwall Minerals Railway. Sections of the original tramway alignment were used but a new line was laid from Ponts Mill north of St. Blazey up the valley under the Treffry Viaduct to re-connect with the course of the old tramway about half a mile beyond.

On 20 July 1960, No. 5539 (St. Blazey) was descending with a china clay train through the valley below the imposing but by then disused Treffry Viaduct. *RCR15156*

Above: As noted earlier all but two of the Cornwall Railway's river crossings made major use of timber. One exception was the Royal Albert Bridge at Saltash; the other was the viaduct at Par which was unique in being 100% built of stone from the start. It is speculated that a timber structure would have been regarded as too insubstantial in an area graced with so many sturdy stone constructions instigated by Joseph Treffry. The result, typical of low railway viaducts throughout the country, is known locally as the "Five Arches". This view was taken on 22 July 1960 looking southwards from the cab of Laira's Warship Class D816 *Eclipse* at the head of a loaded china clay train bound for the Fowey branch. Immediately beyond the level crossing, Par Bridge Crossing Signal Box controlled the junction whereby the Par Harbour line branches off and passes beneath the second arch from the west and curves away to the right beside the public highway. The Fowey branch passed under the viaduct's centre arch and turned in an easterly direction. *RCR15169*

Right: Par viaduct from the south side as 2-8-0T No 4273 (St. Blazey) approaches with china clay empties from Fowey on 23 September 1960. The approach signal is set at danger to protect the junction with the Par Harbour line to the north of the viaduct. For safety purposes, it was normal practice to bring an unfitted freight to a stand before entering a junction or station, prior to being given permission to proceed. *RCR15390*

On Wednesday 6 July 1955, No. 5019 *Treago Castle* of Bristol Bath Road was crossing St. Pinnock viaduct with what Dick Riley recorded as a Glasgow-Penzance working. The inter-regional nature of this train is apparent in the ex-LMS coaching stock but the Train Reporting Number does not accord with a departure from Scotland. TRN 262 in the summer of 1955 was the 12.35 am Monday-Saturday Manchester (London Road)-Plymouth and the Sunday only 1.40 am Crewe-Plymouth. The explanation may be that the Castle, having brought the Manchester train forward from Bristol, was serviced at Laira before taking over the later arrival from Glasgow but without removal of the TRN. Either way, passengers who had started out from Glasgow or Manchester would be looking forward to journey's end. In possible part compensation, there was a view that LMS Period III stock provided the most comfortable ride, provided it was running over Great Western trackwork. Incidentally, "Treago Castle" sounds Cornish but the building is actually a fortified manor house in Herefordshire. *RCR6273*

St. Austell viaduct was about one quarter of a mile to the west of the station on the edge of the town. It was built on a slight left hand curve facing westward and completed in 1858 as a Class A viaduct (height 115', length 720'). It was in service for exactly 40 years until completion of its all-masonry replacement which was built on the Up alongside. It was normal practice for the new viaduct to be built in parallel with the old with the approach tracks slewed over as necessary on approach from either side but this was impossible at the eastern end. The requisite extra land could not be purchased so the new alignment had to curve in across the course of the original route. This resulted in the original masonry plinth embedded in the hillside forming part of the abutment of the new structure, alongside the St. Austell-Bodmin road. Despite efforts to standardise the timber design, special arrangements were necessary with the original structures in relation to the unique characteristics of each location, and also in the manner of their replacement. At St. Austell, seven of the original piers remain in place.

The date is 8 July 1955 and No. 6869 *Resolven Grange* (Laira) is hauling the 10-coach Down "Cornish Riviera" across the viaduct; the distance and the angle make the complete train visible. In its truncated post-war resuscitation programme, the GWR had planned advances in the quality of its services and this was most evident in the Hawksworth-pattern main line coaches. Immediate pre-war coach construction had seen lengths varying between 57' and 60' but Hawksworth's approach was subtly but importantly different. Internal layout and décor did not change significantly but the outer dimensions were now standardised at 64' x 8' 11' so that the extra 4 feet or more made the compartments more spacious. These vehicles were internally very comfortable and definitely superior to the BR Mark 1s that followed. The Hawksworth fleet comprised All First, All Third, Composite, Brake Composite, Brake Third, Passenger Brake types plus four 12-wheeled All First Sleeping Cars. They were subject to experimentation with alternative materials tried for internal finishes, aluminium body panels, and one example had an aluminium chassis to reduce the tare weight. This train is a Hawksworth matched set with a Brake Third at either end but the distance prevents identification of the six All Firsts/ Composites/ All Thirds in the remainder of the rake. The key omission in the GWR's post-war construction programme was any form of catering vehicle. Accordingly, the sixth coach is a Diagram H40 All Third Diner and the seventh, a Diagram H39 First Diner (including kitchen). These 61' 4" bow-ended vehicles were built in 1932 to run as catering pairs – 23 years old and still gracing BR Western Region's premier service. *RCR6336*

Left: This particular train with its distinctive formation has appeared in another album of Dick Riley's work, approaching the Royal Albert Bridge. It is now crossing St. Austell viaduct and the surviving stone piers from the earlier timber structure can be seen just beyond the parapet on the Down side. The 4-6-0, which appears to be a Modified Hall, is approaching Trenance sidings and clay dries to the right of the track. Just less than a mile distant can be seen Gover viaduct which in its timber guise was a Class A example (height 95', length 690'). *RCR7605)*

Bottom: The view of St. Pinnock Viaduct on 6 July 1955 shows how the original Brunel timber structure was modified by building up the original masonry piers to support spans consisting of iron girders. Laira's No 7031 *Cromwell's Castle* is at the head of a modernised Toplight Brake Third following by a pair of Collett All Third bow-ended coaches. *RCR6274)*

Coombe St. Stephens viaduct (Milepost 291¼ Class A, length 738', maximum height 70'), located between Burngullow and Grampound Road, comprised eleven piers set at distances of 64' apart. It was one of the lowest of its type and apparently a contentious structure that was subjected to an arbitration hearing. In original form the line of the viaduct followed a gentle S alignment which Margary regarded as technically unsound, the masonry piers were considered of poor quality, and annual maintenance expenses were higher than the average. For these reasons, the route was re-aligned and a new single track broad gauge viaduct opened in July 1886 to the north of the original. All the masonry stumps of the timber version appear to have remained in situ and presumably their comparatively low height did not necessitate removal as occurred at other locations where substandard workmanship was evident.

Having worked to Penzance the previous day, No. 7031 *Cromwell's Castle* was crossing the viaduct with the Up "Cornish Riviera" on 7th July 1955. As was then customary, the prestige train of the day consisted of a matched set of eight Hawksworth coaches into which was inserted the traditional pair of pre-war catering vehicles. *RCR6296*

Opposite top: In planning the Cornwall Railway, Brunel's standardised design principles had to take account of local topography, as exemplified in valley crossings in the Liskeard area. Four of the tallest viaducts were located over a 5-mile stretch of route at Liskeard (height 150'/ length 720'), Moorswater (147'/ 954'), St. Pinnock (151'/ 633') and Largin (130'/ 567') and three different types of timber structure proved necessary. The timber viaduct at Liskeard (milepost 264½) was completed in 1858 and replaced in 1898. The new structure followed the alignment of the old with brickwork extensions to the original stone piers to support steel girders that carried the trackwork. The join between the stone and brick work can be clearly discerned.

A branch train hauled by a Class 45xx small prairie is in the background, descending into the valley with a service bound for Looe. *RCR6392)*

Opposite bottom: On 16 July 1956, Churchward mogul No. 6305 (St. Blazey) with its Up Type H through freight had just cleared Tresulgan viaduct, halfway between Menheniot and St. Germans. Many freight trains in Cornwall were not unduly heavy and in this case, the composition is 25-30 wagons with a van and two loaded clay hoods leading. Most of the open wagons toward the rear appear to be empty. The pristine nature of the environment is notable with the trackwork in excellent condition and the cutting sides clean with well-tended foliage. Tresulgan timber viaduct (Class A height 93', length 525') was one of the longer-lived. It was replaced in 1899 with this substantial all-stone structure, to the south of the original alignment. *RCR7688*

Above: This view dated 13 July 1956, taken from the driving cab of an auto trailer about to leave Cornwall, reveals that the track work over the Royal Albert bridge was then of conventional ballasted form. It was later replaced with baulk road which was found more efficient at this special location. *RCR76198*

Above: Welcome to Devon!

The Royal Albert Bridge viewed from the footplate of No. 5098 *Clifford Castle* hauling an Up train on 24 September 1960. The train is proceeding under caution, ordained by the fixed distant signal. In the background can be seen the cranes employed in construction of the suspension road bridge and the piers of the new structure on the Devon bank of the Tamar. *RCR15420*

Opposite: On 23 September 1960, the changing motive power scene was evident as No. 4087 *Cardigan Castle* (Laira) passed the small goods yard to the west of Saltash station. The Castle was fitted with a double chimney in February 1958 in a programme that focussed mainly on the youngest class members i.e. the 5098 series. This was the third oldest Castle, and the modification yielded a cost effective improvement in performance. The double chimney programme commenced in May 1956 when No 7018 was fitted with an experimental design, while fitted with a 3-row superheater. This engine, previously regarded as a notably poor performer, had been selected as the guinea pig and it was transformed. Between April 1957 and November 1961, sixty-five more of the class were equipped with a slightly modified chimney style and 4-row superheater. Engines from the 4073, 5013 and 5098 series were selected of which twenty-seven came from the last-named. The cost was modest but full payback was not really achieved as witness No 7021, the last to be modified which was withdrawn a mere 22 months later.

Standing in the Up loop is a three-car DMU with Driving Motor Second No. W51329 leading, which has been allocated to suburban duties centred on Plymouth North Road. This type was built by Birmingham Railway Carriage & Wagon Company in 1960 (later designated Class 118). The unit's condition shows that it has only recently entered service to replace steam-powered auto services.

The stop signal, indicating that the Castle has a clear road, is conventionally located whereas the outer starter comprising home and fixed distant has been placed to the right of the Up line. It was not unusual for GWR signals to be placed on the "wrong" side if it improved sighting for locomotive crews. *RCR15371*

Chapter 2

Main Line

As with so much of the Cornish railway, main line operations had their own distinctive flavour and motive power lacked the variety that could be found east of Plymouth. The Kings were of course banned on account of weight, there were comparatively fewer Castles, and there are no 2-8-0s to be found in this slice of the collection. Main line passenger services connected with the Duchy from points as distant as Glasgow, but motive power for such was drawn mainly from Penzance and Truro sheds plus, inevitably, Plymouth Laira. St. Blazey was less engaged as its activities were orientated more towards servicing freight and china clay traffic. The collection comprises photographs taken between April and September which was understandable as it was a long journey from London to capture sparse out-of-season operations in the shorter hours of daylight. The resultant impression is of a succession of well-filled trains serving England's most remote corner whereas the reality for most of the year was rather different.

The GWR's Timetable dated 6 October 1947 (and until further notice) reveals through service departures for Penzance from Paddington at 5.30 am, 10.30 am (the "Cornish Riviera Express"), 1.30 pm, 9.50 pm and 11.50 pm. Two more services terminated at Plymouth North Road (with a third on Fridays), necessitating a change there to continue westward. This was during the grey austerity years with normality yet to be fully restored to a run-down and exhausted system but the paucity of trains is nonetheless striking. Journey times were impressive for the wrong reasons: the CRE took 7 hours 5 minutes to reach Penzance; the 11.00 am required 8 hours 40 minutes; and the 1.30 pm took 8 hours 20 minutes.

The two night departures included first class sleeping cars (limited availability). In its strenuous efforts to restore normality, the GWR led the Big Four in restoration of on-train catering. All daytime departures for Plymouth and for Penzance included restaurant cars. This just left the notorious 5.30 am from Paddington which avoided the convenience of the Berks and Hants route, went by way of Bristol and crawled into the Cornish terminus 10 hours 55 minutes after leaving London. Any masochist opting for this service would have had to make personal arrangements to stave off thirst or starvation.

In contrast, summer holiday traffic in the 1950s and early 1960s was intense with the running of "extras" at busy times. This was exemplified by the Paddington departures for the Cornish Riviera in the summer of 1955 which were:

Train Reporting No	Departure Time
130	10.30 am Daily (including Sundays)
131	10.35 am As required, Saturdays excepted
133	10.35 am Saturdays only

Both were naturally hauled by Kings but the 10.30 am Saturday working was advertised as Paddington-Truro *non-stop.* How this was achieved is revealed in the Working Timetable which shows a scheduled arrival time of 2.00 pm at Newton Abbot where a seven minute pause ensued. During this interval, the train stood in the yard loop while the King came off to be replaced by a pair of smaller 4-6-0s which then ran on to first stop Truro. Meanwhile, to balance the workings, the King would wait for the following 10.35 am train and join its brother as pilot to North Road, this being the only scheduled working of Kings in tandem. The compiler was at Dainton East one Saturday in 1957 to relish the sight and sound; the 10.30 am was hauled by a Manor and a County

25

Opposite: Not all auto trains that departed westbound from Plymouth North Road terminated at Saltash. These views show an Up auto service departing St. Germans on 16 July 1956, pushed by 0-6-0PT No. 6419 while a Down service arrived the same day hauled by No. 6414. Introduced in February 1932, Class 64xx became a constant feature of Laira's allocation when two months later No. 6406 arrived to stay for its entire career. No. 6414, completed in November 1934, was another that spent its career there, up until withdrawal in June 1959. No. 6419 had been a Laira locomotive since November 1949; it left for Gloucester Horton Road in July 1960.

In the mid-1950s, suburban/ local services based on Plymouth North Road still made use of 70' auto trailers built in 1909 and 1913 to Diagrams Q and R. There were ten in this group and they mainly worked in the Plymouth area although sometimes were also allocated to Exeter. They apparently worked in permanently coupled pairs and were unusual in being provided with corridor connections within each set. The 1913-built vehicles were the last 70 ft auto trailers to be built and the last to have fully panelled wooden bodies. The trailers in these illustrations cannot be positively identified but they do appear to be seventy footers. *RCR7697, 7698*

Above: On 6 July 1955, County Class No. 1006 *County of Cornwall* (Penzance) was approaching Bodmin Road with an Up Falmouth/ Newquay service bound for Paddington. This train comprised solely ex-GWR coaches but in the tradition of its predecessor, BR Western Region often assembled passenger rakes comprising mixed vintages. In this case four vehicles are of the pre-war handsome large-windowed or "Sunshine" stock but the second is a 70' ten compartment All Third of Diagram C44/ 5/ 6 or 50. Known as part of the "South Wales Corridor Stock", Diagrams C44 and C45 were unusual in being bow-ended at one end and flat at the other. The final coach is a Hawksworth Brake Third (D131 or 133). The County is in original condition with boiler pressure of 280 lb/ sq in and single chimney. From the following year, modifications were introduced whereby the pressure was lowered to 250 lb/sq in and a squat double chimney was installed. These changes improved performance and reduced boiler maintenance costs. No. 1006 retained its original chimney until December 1959. *RCR6272*

Opposite: Smartly turned out No. 5098 *Clifford Castle* (a Laira engine from March 1949 until January 1962) stands at Bodmin Road on 24 September 1960 with an Up train. Dick Riley had no trouble in persuading crews to stand by their steeds to be recorded for posterity. Driver and fireman look justifiably proud for the double chimney Castles were fine locomotives as constantly proved in service; No. 5098 was so fitted in January 1959. Pride in the job was infectious in those days, as apparent from the carefully tended flowerbed below the station name board.

The second view shows *Clifford Castle* looking forward and waiting to re-start its journey. The line curving away behind the camera to the left is the start of the branch to Bodmin General. The elaborate gantry arrangement across the two lines on the left supports the water feed to the column in order that locomotives might take water while standing on the Up main. There is a fire devil below the column which has also been used as a mounting point for a modern 9-car stop sign. The starter signal is not in sight but the goods and loop line bracket signal is visible to the left of the junction.

It is not known where Dick Riley joined this train but an earlier view shows this engine tackling Treverrin Bank while later it is about to cross the Royal Albert Bridge. Both photographs were taken from the footplate of No 5098 so presumably he rode on the engine at least as far as Plymouth North Road. *RCR15418, 15419*

Above: At the other end of Bodmin Road on 2 May 1961, a diesel multiple unit was about to depart with a Penzance service. Starting signals for the line to Bodmin General can be seen between the informative platform nameboard and the Up side station buildings. There is plenty of platform activity in evidence on both sides. The water column on the Down side complete with its devil, is considerably less elaborate than its Up counterpart. *RCR15704*

Top: On 9 July 1955, Dick Riley received a friendly wave from the cheerful fireman of No. 1028 *County of Warwick* of Bristol Bath Road as it drew away from Par in the Up direction. The leading vehicle is an inside-frame Siphon G. *RCR6351*

Bottom: No. 4569 (St. Blazey) was waiting in the Newquay branch platform at Par on 9 July 1955, presumably to connect with the arriving Down main line service on the right, in the hands of a 49xx series 4-6-0 Hall. The first two coaches of the main line service are Hawksworth stock, a Diagram D131 or 133 Brake Third leading. The small prairie is in charge of the customary 2-coach B-Set augmented by a BR Suburban Mark 1 All Third. The recessed guard's door suggests that the B-Set is of bow-ender Diagram E145. *RCR6360*

Working under Empty Stock train headcode, Truro's No. 5972 *Olton Hall,* with St. Blazey's 0-6-0PT No. 7715 coupled inside as pilot, was captured north of Middleway Bridge Crossing near St. Blazey on the afternoon of Friday 8 July 1955, bound for Newquay. (Both engines are preserved.) The first coach is a "Sunshine" Brake Composite followed by a BR Mark 1 catering vehicle. Most, if not all, of the remainder of the 12-coach rake are ex-GWR restaurant and dining cars except for what appears to be a Brake Third at the rear. The day of the week is significant as this was part of the pre-weekend summer ritual that saw delivery of such vehicles to Newquay (and other holiday destinations) to be included in the extra trains that would take visitors home the following day. *RCR6343, 6344*

Above: Holiday-bound and nearing its destination on Saturday 9 July 1955, this train is the 5.30 am Paddington-Newquay headed by No. 5972 near Luxulyan. As seen in the preceding view, this engine worked the empty catering vehicles down to Newquay the previous day in preparation for the weekend exodus and is now back with a consignment of holidaymakers bound for the popular resort. The Hall is assisted by Churchward mogul No. 6397 (of St. Blazey), and by a banking locomotive. This heavily loaded 12-coach train shows the splendid variety that could make GWR passenger services so interesting. In this case, a Hawksworth Brake Third leads followed by three Sunshine coaches, a pre-1933 Collett All Third, a Sunshine Composite, a 70' Collett All Third, a Sunshine Brake Third, a Composite Restaurant Car (apparently a 70'/ 71' vehicle of 1923 vintage, Diagrams H26, 28 or 29), a Sunshine Brake Composite, another 70' coach, and finally a Brake Composite. Magnification of Dick Riley's work helps to work out individual types but even without this facility, this view demonstrates the variations in waist and window heights that characterised GWR coaches of different eras.

Opposite: In the second view, the leading engines have passed the cameraman, and the Brake Third can now be confirmed as No W1775W of Diagram D133. Finally, the banking engine, which proves to be small prairie No. 5519 (also of St. Blazey), has passed revealing the last two coaches to be a 70' Toplight All Third and a Sunshine Brake Composite. Despite it being high summer, this service might have been running at or close to schedule as with its early departure time from London, there might have been little delay in negotiating the notorious Taunton to Newton Abbot bottleneck. Saturday services later in the day typically suffered severe hold-ups over that section. In 1959, the compiler recalls turning up at Exeter St. Davids two hours early for the scheduled arrival of a service bringing relatives from Leeds. The train actually steamed in about three hours late – there were worse places to while away five hours on a summer Saturday!

Such traffic congestion provided great entertainment for the enthusiast but these marathons were often the only long distance rail journeys undertaken by many of the travelling public; such experiences damaged passenger perceptions and encouraged investment in a family motor car. *RCR6354, 6355, 6356*

Opposite: The same day (Saturday 9 July 1955) the exodus of holidaymakers returning home from Newquay was also under way. A holiday extra has arrived in the platform loop at Par in the hands of No. 6869 Resolven Grange (a Penzance engine), piloted by locally-allocated large prairie No. 4167. The train, which comprises ex-LMS coaching stock, stretches around the St. Blazey curve, being much longer than Newquay loop platform. In the second view, pilot engine No. 4167 has come off the train and run back onto the goods loop beside the Par transfer shed. Meanwhile, the Grange is blowing off while waiting for the road that will allow continuation of the journey to Plymouth and beyond. *RCR6346, 6347*

Above: Laira's No. 1010 County of Caernarvon made a fine sight on 1 September 1954 climbing away from Par with a Down passenger train of ex-LMS Period III stock. *RCR5397*

Above: A busy scene on the approach to Par on the morning of 6 July 1955. To the right on the Down main, No. 6829 *Burmington Grange* (Newton Abbot) is arriving with an express service, passing No 6809 *Burghclere Grange* (Penzance). The latter is engaged in an empty stock shunting movement for what is thought to be the 11.05 am Par-Penzance stopping train, a summer "extra". The locomotive would have come off St. Blazey shed to drag the stock tender-first out of Chapel (carriage) sidings at the west of station and into the Newquay branch platform. The locomotive would then have run round and propelled the stock out onto the Up main. It seems to be still reversing to clear the trailing crossover. Once the section is clear, it would then cross to the Down main to enter Par and await its scheduled departure. The position of the shadows suggest that the time is around mid-morning. *RCR6271*

Opposite top: Dick Riley was on the footplate of No. 1002 *County of Berks* (St. Blazey) on 23 September 1960. The locomotive is standing with an Up train on the loop at St. Dennis Junction on the Par-Newquay line waiting to cross a Down stopping service comprising a 2-coach B-Set plus a suburban All Third, hauled by a diesel-hydraulic B-B Class D63xx. *RCR15393*

Opposite bottom: No. 4099 *Kilgerran Castle* (Penzance) pounds up the gradient towards Treverrin tunnel with a Down passenger service, passing Treverrin Signal Box at Milepost 279 on 9 July 1955. The ground behind the box formed part of the original Cornwall Railway broad gauge alignment which followed a more twisting route on the climb. Treverrin signal box was opened some time before 1911 and was temporarily closed in November 1914. The date of its reopening is unrecorded but at the time of this photograph final closure was not long off, taking place the following June. Small boxes like this were a common feature of the railway in remote country locations and would only be "switched in" at busy times. The officer in charge would often welcome the company of interested enthusiasts, to relieve the solitude. *RCR6366*

Top: No. 4077 *Chepstow Castle* (Laira) was near Par Harbour with a Down service on Sunday 10 July 1955. The visible coaching stock comprises a Sunshine All Third, a Collett Brake Third, and another Sunshine vehicle. The line in the foreground climbed steeply behind the camera to connect with the main line, thus providing alternative access to the docks without having to negotiate the St. Blazey complex. The barrel-shaped building to the right behind the timber structure was the engine shed that housed two 0-4-0ST shunters, *Judy* and *Alfred*, that worked the dock lines. *RCR6372*

Bottom: Not all summer "extras" were for holidaymakers. On Sunday 10 July 1955, No. 5918 *Walton Hall* with banking assistance had begun the climb away from St. Blazey up the Luxulyan Valley with a Bradford-Newquay troop special. From what can be seen of the train, at least part of the stock seems to be LMS Period II. *RCR6373*

Opposite: A busy morning with three pending departures at Penzance station, all in the hands of Diesel-Hydraulic locomotives. The train on the left is headed by a pair of North British-built "baby Warships", Nos. D6314 and D6306. Although not a particularly successful class, their varied duties underlined the flexibility that diesel power promised. They were used on pick-up goods work, they replaced small prairies at the head of 2-coach B-Sets on branch services, and when working in multiple, they took on express passenger trains as in this case. This picture is believed to be from 9 April 1959, with confirmation from the next train to the right with the Train Reporting Number 962 on the D8xx B-B Warship. The year 1959 was the last in which all-number 3-digit TRNs were used as the next year, the system changed to 3-digit alpha-numeric designations. In 1959, this TRN referred to the 12.00 noon Monday-Saturday Penzance-Manchester. The D8xx Warship on the right is also carrying a TRN but it is too distant to decipher.

This panorama offers a window on the motive power future but tradition remains in evidence. The coaches of the left-hand and centre trains are BR Mark 1s but the first vehicle behind the two baby Warships is a Siphon G. Two Cordons are parked on the short stub siding in the centre background and the platforms' gas lighting is one reason for their presence. In the right background stands the dingy train shed which always seemed a long way from Paddington's splendour, as indeed it was by mileage. *RCR14617*

Above: Return journey. At 1.55 pm, 12 July 1956 No. 1006 *County of Cornwall* (appropriately allocated to Penzance from September 1955 to July 1960) was departing from that station with a passenger service bound for Newton Abbot. This is another train with a mixture of Great Western stock. The six vehicles in sight are three pre-war large-windowed coaches (Brake 3rd/ All 3rd/ Composite), an earlier Collett All 3rd., an unidentified coach and then what seems to be a Toplight Brake coach. It is not clear whether the train consists of any more coaches but if it is just this five, then this was hardly a demanding duty for a County. *RCR7608*

Chapter 3

Branch Line

Having travelled Down the main line to Penzance in the previous chapter, return eastwards is by way of the passenger branch lines that were open in the 1950s and early 1960s. In Dick Riley's time, the stations at St. Erth, Gwinear Road, Chacewater, Truro, Par, Lostwithiel, Bodmin Road, and Liskeard served as junctions for a network of passenger branch lines that connected with the Plymouth-Penzance artery. The Par-Newquay route might be termed a branch but in addition to its local services, it handled heavy china clay traffic and a number of long distance passenger services.

These bucolic byways had an especial charm and offered the discerning explorer the opportunity to see beautiful countryside not normally accessible by road. Tourist trade during the summer months could require addition of a "strengthener" coach but for the remainder of the year, a two-vehicle formation usually sufficed to provide a service ample for local community needs.

From 1960 onwards, this rural network started to undergo change with closure of surplus sidings and introduction of small diesel locomotives. The latter's presence was short-lived as the GWR's classic passenger stock soon yielded to first generation diesel multiple units, even before Dr Beeching had his say. It is indeed fortunate therefore that Dick Riley was able to capture the spirit of a friendly, intimate local steam railway scene that had been embedded in the community since the 19th Century, but which would not last for much longer.

--- o O o ---

Opposite: The St. Ives branch has been traditionally associated with holiday passengers but from its opening as a broad gauge route in 1877, it delivered a wide variety of general merchandise and exported significant tonnages of locally landed fish. The catch was loaded at the far end of the curved passenger platform. This traffic had suffered progressive decline by the mid-20th Century and goods services were withdrawn in 1963. The branch was then marked for complete closure in the Beeching Report but gained a reprieve. Modernisation saw replacement of the attractive station facilities with a simple straight platform line. The treatment worked and at the time of writing, the route not only survives but sees 28 departures from St. Erth every weekday.

Long before modernisation, small prairie No. 4563 of Penzance was passing behind St. Erth Signal Box on 12 July 1956 having departed from the St. Ives bay on its 4¼-mile journey. The box faced southward with the Penzance-Plymouth main line immediately in front and comparison with the earlier view of Truro East Box shows how these structures could differ. This is an all-brick building, more correctly labelled "SIGNAL BOX" on the rear side (and also on the front). The finial-bedecked roof is gabled in this case and the style of window frames is quite different, but the whole ensemble is instantly recognisable as GWR. The normal composition for the branch train was a 2-coach B-Set which in this case appears to be a pair of maroon Collett bow-ended Brake Composites of Diagram E145 (note the recessed guard's doors). To help with heavier summer traffic, a Collett corridor All Third in blood and custard livery has been added; the angle prevents confirmation of its diagram. *RCR7611*

Above: On 9 April 1960, No 4566 (Penzance) was on the St. Ives duty and is entering St. Erth with a B-set comprising two 57' Diagram E116 Brake Composites. These coaches had an unusual layout where the First Class compartments were in-board, i.e. immediately adjacent at the centre of the set. Each coach had seven compartments, which was achieved through a significantly shorter van section than with other diagrams. Meanwhile 0-6-0PT No. 1650, also of Penzance (a short-term resident from March to July 1960), is shunting a travel-worn cattle wagon in front of the creamery. The tracks of the Penzance-Plymouth line are in the foreground. *RCR14643*

Opposite page: Dick Riley was on the footplate of small prairie No. 4564 between St. Erth and St. Ives on 24 September 1960. (This engine had reputedly moved from Penzance to Shrewsbury engine shed in December 1959, obviously a case of mis-recording.) In the first view, the train has just departed from St. Erth. Shortly after the ground signal, the route became single; the right hand line and the sidings were taken out of use in 1964. At this point, the main line curves away to the right behind the trees. The second image shows that the first stop on the branch was all of one mile away at Lelant, hard against the Hayle Estuary. The branch was the last to be built to broad gauge and at the time, the modest quay to the extreme right was sufficiently busy to justify its own siding. *RCR15408, 15411*

Above: The original St. Ives branch terminus was an attractive curved station, close to town and sea, and a great favourite with the modelling community. On the same day as the two previous views, No. 4564 in lined green livery has run-round and is ready to return to St. Erth. Judging by the body language of those on the platform, and the coach's open doors, departure will be a little time yet. *RCR15407*

Opposite: The location is Helston, England's most southerly railhead, and the date is 24 September 1960. Small prairie No. 4563 (Penzance) was on duty that day with a B-Set consisting of two Diagram E116 Brake Composites. The footplate crew seem proud of their responsibilities. By this date, the prairie had been in service almost 36 years, and withdrawal would come some 13 months later. A sign of late life repairs is the prominent horizontal weld line along the side tank where a wasted panel had been replaced. Duties like this would soon be taken over by "baby Warship" D63xx diesel-hydraulic locomotives.

Dick Riley was allowed into the cab of No. 4563 to take the second photograph of Helston station yard and throat. Yet another of his panoramas that reveals so much of the minutiae of the steam branch line railway, confirming that twelve years after nationalisation the GWR lived on in a host of details. *RCR15414, 15415*

Above: Chacewater station photographed from a departing Down train on 8 April 1960 with Truro's small prairie No. 5515 standing in the Newquay loop with its local train. The Newquay-Chacewater route was authorised in 1897 and completed in 1905 as a late addition to the GWR's Cornish network. It was intended to meet the needs of an area with inadequate rail connections and also to discourage the London & South Western's aspirations to penetrate that corner of the county. Construction required 12 miles of new line plus the up-grade of five miles of goods-only route at the Newquay end, built by the Cornwall Minerals Railway. Branch passenger services started from Chacewater and paralleled the Cornwall main line for about half a mile in a westerly direction before turning northwards at the triangular Blackwater Junction. The steeply graded route went by way of St. Agnes to come close to the sea at Perranporth Beach and then Perranporth itself before joining the line from Par at triangular Tolcarn Junction, a little more than a mile from Newquay. *RCR14612*

Traffic was never heavy apart from seasonal summer custom and the route was closed in 1963. On 23 September 1960, No. 5537 (Truro) in lined green was standing at Perranporth with a train bound for Chacewater while a service in the opposite direction has also arrived at the island platform. The small prairie's train comprised a "blood and custard" All Third Diagram C67 and a pair of maroon-liveried coaches. The centre vehicle is partly obscured by the water column but it might be a Diagram D124 Brake Third, a type distinguished by the door-less droplight windows in the corridor. At the far end of the set is what appears to be an earlier vintage All Third. A secondary service such as this often used cascaded main line stock of an earlier era; the differing body styles, waist and window heights added to the visual variety. *RCR15394, 15396*

This undated view depicts Penwithers Junction looking eastwards in the direction of Truro (the nearby hamlet is known as Penweathers). The Penzance-Truro section of the Cornish main line curves in from the left and then proceeds straight towards the 70-yard long Higher Town Tunnel, followed by descent into Truro station. This photograph was taken from the veranda of the Toad of a train bound for the Newham branch. The small prairie has left the train on the Falmouth branch which became single behind the camera, has run round and is now reversing up before taking the train down two-mile elongated S-course of the freight-only branch to reach the wharves beside the Truro River. The positioning of the two home signals that protect the junction calls for comment. That on the left is apparently sited to improve its sighting for approaching Up trains on the left-hand curve while the placement of that on the right reduces the chance of it being mistaken for its nearby companion.

The Newham branch and terminus marked the eastern extent of the standard gauge West Cornwall Railway which was formed in 1846 to absorb and up-grade the industrial Hayle Railway. New sections were built between Redruth and Truro, and between Hayle and Penzance with completion of the Newham-Penzance link in 1852. The Cornwall Railway (which had opened to Truro in May 1859) completed a broad gauge extension to Penwithers in 1860, and opened the Falmouth branch in 1863. Faced with a shortage of indigenous traffic, the break-of-gauge at Penwithers, and the obligation to make mandatory improvements to its facilities, the WCR did not prosper. It was acquired by the "associated companies" (GWR plus Bristol & Exeter and South Devon railways) in 1865. Following conversion of the Penzance section to dual gauge and extensive remodelling of Penwithers Junction, the Newham branch closed to passengers in 1863. It remained open for goods traffic until 1971. RCR15161

Above: Truro's No. 5744 climbs away from its home location on 22 July 1960 with its "busby" in place on a branch service to Falmouth. The spark arrester is reputed not to have affected steaming; this equipment is discussed in connection with this locomotive's "naked" condition in Chapter 5. *RCR15199*

Opposite top: By 11 July 1961, diesel units had displaced steam-hauled passenger trains on the Falmouth branch but freight traffic still remained steam-hauled. Class 8750 No. 3709 is distinguished by its stump of a chimney, similar to that on No. 5744 seen elsewhere in this volume.

The pannier is drawing from the docks branch a string of wagons comprising three closed vans, three containers loaded on what appear to be Conflats of Diagrams H6 to H11, an ex-SR van, two empty 4-wheel long wheelbase flat wagons, another container and at least six petroleum tank wagons. With no sign of a brake van, this must be a shunting movement. The access line to the extensive dockyard railway complex curves away to the left behind the white shed; a short rake of coaches is standing on the adjacent loop.

Encroaching vegetation in the foreground presages removal of remaining locomotive servicing facilities of which the siding with the water column and tank were the last vestige (taken out of use in May 1964). The two road engine shed and turntable had been removed by 1927. *RCR16074*

Opposite bottom: No. 6809 *Burghclere Grange* (allocated to Penzance) was heading a local service from Newquay to Plymouth near Roche on 8 July 1955. From another photograph in the portfolio, it is apparent that this train comprised a 2-coach B-set plus another vehicle which might have been a corridor coach. *RCR6399*

Above: On 8 July 1955, 0-6-0PT No. 9673 (a St. Blazey engine from March 1951 until withdrawal in May 1960) was passing St. Dennis Junction with the 6.25 pm Par-Newquay local passenger comprising four non-corridor coaches. This was a busy junction where two goods-only routes converged with the Newquay line. That immediately to the right of the signal box led to Drinnick Mill and then wended its way southwards to connect with the Cornwall Railway main line at Burngullow. The next line to the right which curves around behind the rake of china clay wagons on the siding is the start of the 4-mile Retew branch that terminated at Meledor Mill. This area is at the heart of the china clay industry as apparent by the mounds of waste in the distance. *RCR6341*

Opposite top: This portrait of St. Blazey Station was taken from the Newquay end, an unusual angle. The siding used for coach storage is to the immediate left. The large building in the distance behind the facing signal is the wagon shop. Behind the cluster of wagons can be seen the rear of the gables of the unique roundhouse shed and then the shed extension building which encompassed the civil engineers' workshops at the far end. Moving further right is St. Blazey Signal Box which was moved to the Down platform in 1908 from its earlier location on the Up side. This box controlled the junction between the Par Loop and the line that later split towards Par docks and Fowey; it also directed access to St. Blazey yards. To the right of the box stands the remains of the station buildings. The crumbling platforms are still in place revealing the extension to the Down platform installed in 1894 (the Up platform was similarly treated then). To the right beyond the station (which closed completely in 1934) can be seen the fan of goods sidings installed in 1909/10. Out of shot a few yards to the right, the double track became single for the remainder of the route to Newquay. Dick Riley spent a lot of his holiday time around the Par-St. Blazey complex and it is easy to see why as this location was host to the most diverse patterns of traffic and motive power in the county. *RCR5402*

Opposite bottom: No. 5564 (St. Blazey) was leaving the Par loop past St. Blazey yard on its way to Newquay at the head of a local service on 17 July 1960. This being summer, the train's capacity has been increased with the addition of a suburban All Third of Diagram C66 or C75. *RCR15091*

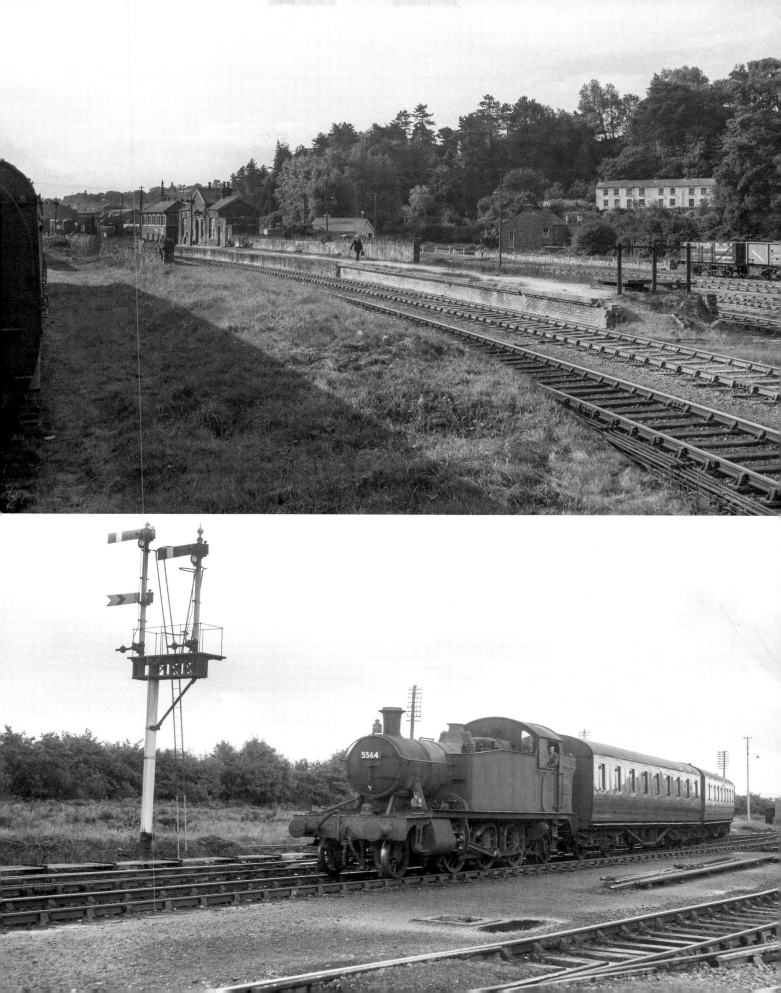

Above: Churchward mogul No. 6309 was rounding the Par loop and about to enter the station on 2 September 1954 with a service from Newquay. The train (a matched set of three Hawksworth coaches:- Brake Third, Composite and All Third in that order) is traversing the facing crossover on the loop to enter the Newquay platform of Par station. This locomotive was a short-term St. Blazey resident, arriving from Gloucester in February 1954 and departing to Swindon shed the following September. *RCR5364*

Opposite: On 2 September 1954, 0-4-2T No. 1419 (a long time St. Blazey resident) was standing in Fowey station with the auto service for Lostwithiel. This was the only regular duty for Class 14xx in the county as compared with Devon where these engines performed over a variety of routes. Between December 1928 and April 1933, the GWR built 32 auto trailers to Diagrams A27, A28 and A30 and they were an interesting blend of old and new. Their internal layout was entirely traditional but they were the first purpose-designed auto-trailers to have all-steel bodies while maintaining the Toplight tradition. They were built with end-windows to the luggage area although by then, experience must have proven with older vehicles that this feature was prone to damage from coal dislodged from the locomotive's bunker. The windows were later replaced with steel panels as in this case. There were detail differences between the three diagrams and this coach is either A27 or A28, the body of the latter being three feet longer at 62' 6" according to the diagram, although the official length was 62' 8". The main difference lay in the length of the saloons as reflected in window spacings but otherwise the two types were identical.

The station had already undergone a measure of rationalisation by this date. In GWR days there had been three lines with that on the left serving as arrival platform, the centre being used by Fowey-St. Blazey china clay traffic while that on the right was for passenger departures. The latter platform was closed in September 1948 and the track removed; the dilapidated remains of the station building can still be seen. In the background, the goods yard is still in business with timber-bodied wagons loaded with coal in evidence.

In the second view, No. 1419 is on its way towards Lostwithiel passing the extensive sidings that served Fowey docks. The vessel in the background is the *Maria Victoria*, engaged in loading china clay. Moored off-shore towards the left is a motor launch of the Royal Air Force Marine Branch. These vessels were stationed around the coastal waters of the UK and were officially designated "Rescue and Target Towing Launches". The origins of the Marine Branch go back to World War 1 but the exploits of vessels of the size and general configuration of that depicted are best recalled for their effectiveness in recovering downed pilots under hazardous and dangerous conditions in the English Channel during the later conflict. This unusual branch of the RAF was disbanded in 1986 when its duties were taken over by Air Sea Rescue helicopters and the RNLI/ Coastguard.

Back on shore, No 1419 will take around 15 minutes to cover the 8½ miles to Lostwithiel including a pause at Golant Halt, roughly the halfway point, beside the River Fowey. *RCR5389, 5391*

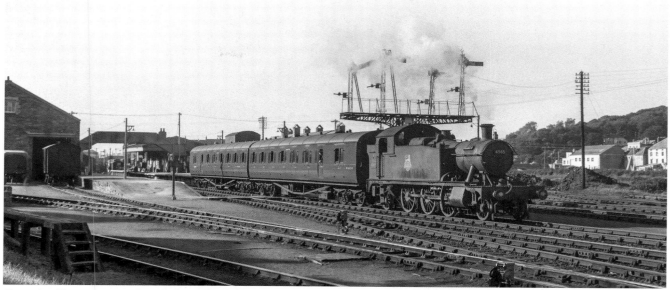

Opposite: The archetypal Cornish branch passenger train formation in the 1950s was a 2-6-2T Class 45xx/ 4575 and a 2-coach B-Set. On 3 September 1954, No. 4584 (St. Blazey) was entering Bodmin General with a pair of Diagram E145 bow-ended Composite Brakes. This type was built between September 1932 and February 1933 as almost the last examples of the Collett bow-ender era, excluding the Centenary Stock. In the second view, the B-set has been stowed alongside the platform and the engine has run round to await departure. The starting signal bracket for trains to Bodmin Road (left) and Wadebridge (right) is a mixture of original contractor and Great Western standard fittings. *RCR5409, 5410*

Above: On 31 August 1954 No 4585 (St. Blazey) was leaving Wadebridge under "foreign" signals with the 5.35 pm for Bodmin Road. The first coach of the B-Set is numbered W6412W which confirms its Diagram as E140. Pairs of coaches forming B-Sets often had consecutive numbers and many stayed monogamous throughout their careers. Vehicle No W6411W shared the same construction and withdrawal dates (August 1930 and June 1959) and so is likely to have formed the other half of this train.

In the first stage of modernisation in Cornwall, "baby Warship" diesel-hydraulics of Class D63xx replaced small prairies on branch services while the B-Sets were retained. However that combination was short-lived following introduction of the ubiquitous diesel multiple unit which soon rendered non-corridor locomotive-hauled passenger stock redundant. Most of diagram E140 were withdrawn in 1959/60; set Nos W6409/ 6410W survived until March 1962. *RCR5364*

Bottom: For many years three venerable ex-LSWR Beattie 2-4-0WTs had been allocated to Wadebridge to work the Wenford minerals branch. In 1962, they were replaced by three members of ex-GWR 0-6-0PT Class 1366. They had previously worked the Weymouth harbour branch and Wadebridge was to be their last home in normal service as follows: No. 1367 in August 1962, withdrawn October 1964; No. 1368 (May 1962 – October 1964); No. 1369 (August 1962 – November 1964, and then preserved). No. 1368 had yet to be joined by its fellows when seen engaged in carriage shunting at Wadebridge on 21 June 1962. *RCR16535*

Top: No. 4552 (St. Blazey) was awaiting departure from the terminus section of Liskeard station with a service bound for Looe by means of the Extension Railway on 17 July 1960. The platform (still in situ today) is at right angles to those of the through station. The connecting line curved around behind the photographer's position and trailed on to the Down main towards the right. The Liskeard and Looe Extension Railway gained Royal Assent in July 1895 and was completed in May 1901, thus finally connecting the Looe-Moorswater-Caradon line with the national network.

The train comprises a classic collection of Collett era coaches, the first of which is bow-ended Diagram D109 Suburban 61' Brake Third No W6527W, built August 1931 and withdrawn February 1962. The other two coaches are slightly older being bow-ended 58' Diagram C54 All Thirds, a type built in significant numbers between 1925 and 1929. *RCR15086*

Bottom: The same rake of coaches and presumably the same locomotive was later captured climbing the Extension Railway from Coombe Junction to Liskeard. This photograph appears to have been taken from an Up train crossing Liskeard Viaduct. The prairie will shortly commence to turn left through 180 degrees to continue its climb up to the branch terminus. *RCR15084*

Chapter 4

Goods train

The motive power profile for freight traffic was less complex than east of Plymouth and was concentrated mainly in the hands of six-coupled locomotives. Judging by the composition of the collection, Castles (of the single chimney variety) seemed to be favourites for parcels and perishables traffic while Counties often appeared with milk trains. By the late 1950s, Granges, which seemed ideal for local conditions, formed the backbone of main line traffic, fulfilling a genuine mixed traffic role. They progressively dislodged Class 43xx as the older 2-6-0s were whittled away.

Shorter distance work resided as elsewhere in the hands of prairies and panniers. Larger 2-6-2Ts were useful on main line freight services as station to station distances were not great. On branch duties, the smaller prairies held sway on both freight and passenger trains, assisted on occasion by members of the 57xx pannier family.

Eight -coupled tender engines were rare; there was an occasional visit by Class 28xx/ 2884 and a Stanier 8F was allocated to Penzance for a time during the war. 2-8-0T Class 42xx was ideal for working china clay trains to Par and Fowey, and as far east as Plymouth. 2-8-2T No 7209 also worked with the St. Blazey contingent from July 1950 to October 1952 plus Nos 7200, 7220 & 7236 for short spells in 1952.

Rendered superfluous by nearby Par which was better situated to handle main line, Newquay branch and exchange traffic, St. Blazey station was located to the north of the motive power depot and yard. It closed to passengers in 1925, and to workmen's trains in 1934. The loop from Par as far as this station was double track but the Newquay branch was single from there onwards. Sufficient use was still being made of the Down side station buildings just visible to the left to warrant retention of traditional fire buckets. On the Up line only the overgrown platform remains where some redundant sleepers have been deposited. A small mystery is the partly obscured milepost which seems to read 281¼ whereas that at the eastern end of Par station stated 281¾. The carriage siding to the right, which trailed into the Up line of the Par loop, contains three Hawksworth-era suburban coaches plus what might be a panelled auto coach at the far end. The junction between the loop and the line that led to Par Harbour and the Fowey branch was controlled by a signal box placed at the southern end of the Down platform. The train is passing through the station running "wrong road" to facilitate handover of the single line token, before passing through the facing points immediately beyond that will allow entry to the Up line to proceed to Par. Alternatively, the locomotive had reversed its train out of the yard and has been given the road to depart eastwards. The Down line was bi-directionally signalled and the bracket signal acted as starter

The date is 10 July 1961 and GWR moguls were by then becoming thin on the ground. The 43xx series had gone, only about a dozen of the 53s remained, and the later Churchward engines were suffering attrition. No. 7335 (of Laira) which dated from March 1932 had started life as one of Collett's up-rated 93xx series with side window cab and detail improvements. The modifications made them heavier, necessitating their placement in the Red route availability category. Originally numbered 9313, further changes in August 1958 reduced the weight making it a "Blue" engine, hence the renumbering. No. 7335 was a St. Blazey resident from at least 1959 but was withdrawn from Gloucester in September 1963. It was coupled to one of the "intermediate" 3500 gallon tenders numbered 2374-83 built in 1925/ 6. The locomotive is carrying the head code for mineral or empty wagon trains.
RCR16066

Opposite top: On 10 July 1961, locally allocated 0-6-0PT No. 9655 was drawing a goods train (headcode is pick-up or branch goods) off the Par loop into the closed St. Blazey station. It is probable that the train will then be reversed onto the Par Harbour/ Fowey line to gain access to the goods yard. This was either [i] a transfer working from Par [ii] a local goods that might have started its journey at Lostwithiel or [iii] an Up goods arrival at Par, which has been dragged back with train locomotive still attached around the loop bound for remarshalling in St. Blazey yard. The latter process was often used to avoid running round in the Par station environs. Today's block freight trains lack the variety that gave a goods train so much interest in the early 1960s. Immediately behind the pannier is a fitted 5-plank open wagon followed by a locally based Toad and then four tank wagons owned by Imperial Chemical Industries. The first is a modern vehicle but the other three are significantly older. When new, No 9655 went to St. Blazey on 28 December 1946 where it stayed until transfer to Pontypool Road on 19 May 1962. It was withdrawn in May 1964. *RCR16068*

Opposite bottom: The notes accompanying the collection are brief and non-existent in the case of this photograph which is a pity as it would be nice to know what is going on. The location is just north of Coombe Junction on the line between Moorswater and Looe and No. 4526 (St. Blazey), having run around its train, is about to proceed down the valley to Looe, or to start the 1 in 40 climb to Liskeard. The short goods train has a Toad at either end to facilitate the run-round process either at Coombe or further up the valley at Moorswater, and judging by the number of personnel in attendance this might be a permanent way working. One of the gentlemen aboard the train has the air of an unofficial passenger. Such matters were more relaxed in those days. Beyond the bridge stands another small prairie, presumably waiting for the Coombe section to clear before going about its duties while in the background, a 2-cylinder 4-6-0 (Hall or Grange) crosses Moorswater viaduct with a Down passenger service. *RCR5358*

Above: Doublebois, halfway between Liskeard and Bodmin Road, and No. 6826 *Nannerth Grange* (Penzance) is cantering westwards on 10 July 1961 with a short rake of vans under pick-up or branch goods head code. A travelling crane is standing behind the Down platform shelter on the head shunt that served the fan of sidings visible to the east of the station. These were installed by the War Department in 1943 and were operated by the Admiralty until 1954 when BR took them over for permanent way purposes. A pannier tank in the far distance is working in these sidings.

The crane is almost certainly a unique example in BR Western Region's fleet. Numbered GW No. 75 (later BR DW75) with a 15-ton capacity, it was purchased from Joseph Booth Ltd of Rodley (Leeds) in February 1927. Allocated initially to Cardiff Docks, it was later with the Engineer's Departments at Newport, Neath and then Swindon from where it was withdrawn in the early 1970s. The Hybar wagon contains coal for the crane to which it is coupled. This is labelled *Empty to Newport* which was presumably where the ensemble was based at this time. It is not clear why it was so far from home. *RCR16071*

Above: On 31 August 1954, 0-6-0PT No. 7709 was propelling wagons from St. Blazey yard down the branch to Par harbour. Par viaduct, in the background, was the only all-stone viaduct on the Cornwall Railway's main line when it opened in 1859. Although later associated with china clay, local business man Joseph Treffry developed Par Harbour in the early 19th Century to handle export of copper ore. He converted the River Par from Pontsmill, a mile to the north of St. Blazey, into a canal to facilitate movement of ore and later constructed a tramway for a similar purpose. The viaduct, built to cross canal and tramway, was known locally as "Five Arches". At the time of this photograph, the road to the harbour passed under the left hand arch while the next accommodated a footpath and the port branch. The third crossed the Fowey branch and the signals that controlled the approach to the junction with the harbour line can be seen through the arch with co-acting repeaters on the tall post above. This junction was controlled by Par Bridge Crossings Signal Box.

No. 7709 was built in March 1930 by Kerr, Stuart (Builder's No. 4444). It was first allocated to Old Oak Common followed by several moves around the London Division before transfer in July 1945 to St. Blazey from where it was withdrawn in August 1960. RCR5349

Opposite top: This was recorded as an Up train of freight empties near Polperro Tunnel on 7 July 1955, hauled by one of St. Blazey shed's 2-8-0Ts, in this case No. 4206. The wagon on the left, labelled "Empty to Menheniot", is a Diagram P7 hopper ballast wagon of which over 400 were built between 1893 and 1901. The capacity was originally 12 tons but later increased to 20 tons by vertical body extensions of about one foot. This wagon type revolutionised the unloading of ballast during permanent way work. Marshalled in rakes ahead of contemporary Diagram AA5 Ballast Ploughs/ Brake Vans, they substantially reduced the need for manual labour; some of diagram P7 were also equipped with their own ballast spreaders. They proved especially useful during replacement of longitudinal baulk track with the cross-sleeper version, following abolition of the broad gauge. The next five 20-ton wagons are to Diagram P22, and built with all welded bodies from 1945 into BR days. RCR6304

Opposite bottom: No. 5915 Trentham Hall was in charge of a Down unfitted express freight comprising about a dozen wagons approaching Polperrow Tunnel between Grampound Road and Truro on 7 July 1955. Halls were the common 4-6-0 workhorse throughout BR Western Region except in Cornwall where Granges were preferred. This was presumably on account of their smaller driving wheel diameter and improved steam passages which imparted that extra punch in hill climbing. No. 5915 differed in having moved to Penzance shed before 1947, and it remained allocated there until September 1956 when it was transferred to Reading. RCR6305

Opposite: These two views give an insight into the shunting movements necessary to add or detach the tankers of milk trains between the West Country and London. On 12 July 1956, No. 1002 *County of Berks* (Penzance) has arrived at St. Erth and run on to the St. Ives branch before setting back into the sidings that served the United Dairies depot. The Passenger Brake Van has been shunted into the left hand siding and detached; its end profile can just be detected behind the locomotive's outside steam pipe. The County then ran back onto the branch and reversed into the right-hand of the two sidings, where it is now standing, to collect loaded tank wagons.

The process was then reversed to collect the Passenger Brake Van and in the second view the ensemble is now backing off the St. Ives branch to return to the Up main line within the confines of St. Erth station. Once clear of the branch junction, the County will be free to continue its course towards Plymouth and London. The train can now be seen to comprise seven 6-wheel milk tankers and a PBV which appears to be of Diagram K41 or K42. At this stage, this comparatively short train would have weighed around 230 tons but probably became substantially heavier by the time it reached Plymouth. *RCR7610, 7612*

Above: Churchward mogul No. 6397 (St. Blazey) was nearing Trerule Signal Box on a Down through unfitted freight on 16 July 1956. The train consists of around 15 wagons of which the final pair in front of the Toad (balcony leading) seem to be 4 or 5 plank opens. The remainder are standard 16 ton BR mineral wagons and around four timber-bodied 7-plank opens. Nothing can be seen of the load but there is a strong probability that it was locomotive coal. The cost of moving fuel over significant distances from South Wales was a significant element in the railway's operating economics in the far west. *RCR7692*

Two views were taken at St. Germans of Up fitted van trains on 16 July 1956. The first was hauled by No. 6873 *Caradoc Grange* (Laira) and the second by No. 5943 *Elmdon Hall* (Laira). Just east of this station, the main line deviated south of the original alignment of the single line Cornwall Railway, crossed the delightfully named River Tiddy and then swung northwards. The new double track route, which was progressively introduced between 1905 and 1908, took the railway away from the shoreline of the Lynher River, a tributary of the Tamar, and allowed demolition of the Forder, Wivelscombe and Grove timber viaducts. The deviation reconnected with the old route just before Defiance Platform, a halt one mile west of Saltash. *RCR7699, 7700*

Above: The year 1960 is regarded as the last in which steam was in abundance in the west which makes this portrait dated 29 April 1961 of Castle Class No. 5053 *Earl Cairns* (a Laira engine) at Penzance shed particularly pleasing. The impression is given of a crew in charge of a smartly-maintained locomotive with a light patina of grime, all ready for imminent action. The engine has the later style of outside steam pipes and a Hawksworth tender whose smooth welded construction contrasts with the cab-side rivets. Someone has left a cloth on the running plate in front of the rear splasher and a section of brass beading is missing from the leading splasher. Small blemishes that detract not one iota from the much-loved style of a genuine working steam engine in everyday condition.

Castles were significantly outnumbered by their 2-cylinder 4-6-0 brethren in the far west. No. 5053's progress to Plymouth might thus have turned some heads. How many would have noticed the disparity in diameters between that of the nameplate and its attendant splasher, a legacy of its original home on "Dukedog" 5' 8" 4-4-0 No 3210? *RCR15659*

Opposite top: As indicated in the shed allocation summaries above, Classes 45xx and 4575 feature prominently in this album being ideal for local and branch services. No. 4564 was standing in Truro shed yard on 20 July 1960; Dick Riley took several photographs of this locomotive on that occasion and its condition is clearly the reason. Repainting of secondary passenger locomotives in lined mid-chrome green was a hallmark of Western steam's glorious Indian Summer. This sentimental livery perhaps looked its very best on the small prairies; this engine had been in plain black until very shortly before this photograph.

Although shed allocations in the 1950-60 period are well documented, inconsistencies do occur in the records and No. 4564 is a case in point. Some records suggest that this engine moved from Cornwall to Shrewsbury in December 1959 whereas the Engine Record Card indicates that it was on Penzance's books from 21 February 1959 until 5 September 1963 when it was transferred to Gloucester. Its presence at Truro in July 1960 and the 83G shed code plate supports the latter contention.

The condition of the locomotive suggests that it had recently undergone an overhaul which, unless this was a programmed Heavy General, would have most likely been undertaken at Newton Abbot. *RCR15165*

Opposite Bottom: Running bunker first, small prairie No. 4549 (of Penzance) was coasting down the gradient past Truro shed, leading baby Warships Nos. D6316 and D6312 (both Laira allocated and then four and five months old respectively) with an Up service on 22 July 1960. During the transition phase, mixed power combinations were common and a steam locomotive at the front would evoke cries of derision from youthful enthusiasts, assuming yet another diesel failure. In the early stages of its short career, North British Class D63xx was not noted for high standards of reliability but in this case, attachment of the prairie would seem to have been for positioning purposes rather than as a rescue operation. *RCR15197*

Pilot duties completed, grubby No. 4549 is running back through Truro station, bound for the shed. A long-term resident of Machynlleth, this engine moved to Laira (February 1960), to Penzance (June 1960) and to Truro (August 1960) from where it was withdrawn the following month. The front end reveals that the smokebox number plate has been removed and only the lugs remain. The buffer beam number was applied by a skilled Launceston fireman in time-honoured fashion while the engine was on Laira's books (he gave similar treatment to No 4591). Why the cast number plate had been removed is not known but it was purchased around 1965 by the impecunious compiler for the vast sum of 7s 6d at the Great Western Society's Totnes depot. If memory serves, Swindon was disposing of cab-side plates for £7 10s and name plates for £15 each in the mid-1960s. Purchase of a genuine GWR plate lay beyond the dreams of avarice but smokebox 4549 remains a treasured possession to this day. Penzance retained some of Class 45xx for working the St. Ives branch until the end of steam on that route as the 4575 series were precluded on account of their being four tons heavier. *RRCR15203*

Above: Another of the county's small prairie tribe, No. 4563 of Penzance, stands outside Helston sub-Shed on 24 September 1960. This compact building was approached from the platform road and located adjacent to the station throat just as the route to Helston curved away to the right – an ideal prototype for modelling purposes. There was a small office attached to the shed building, two small coal stages and a water tower. Covered accommodation was sufficient for one prairie which was just as well because, unlike other sub-sheds serving points off the Cornwall main line, the allocation was a single locomotive. *RCR15413*

Bottom: The panoramic view of Truro shed taken on 8 April 1960 shows that steam still dominates, but not for much longer. A sign of change is the composition of the small prairies on parade. All four are of the 4575 version as by the previous summer the older 45xx variety was in the minority at Cornish depots. A Grange is standing to the extreme left and what looks like another is on the left-hand shed road. To the left a 94xx pannier and another 4-6-0 are largely hidden by the hut and the vans on the siding. *RCR14602*

Above: Truro depot was situated in what resembled a natural bowl in the hill but was actually a man-made excavation, the spoil being used to level land occupied by the northern and eastern sides of the yard and station site. Smartly-presented single chimney No 1018 *County of Leicester* was on its home shed on 12 July 1956. The Counties were something of a Marmite type, criticised by many observers but the compiler admits to having liked them. They exuded a measure of modernity as a symbol of the stunted aspirations of a post-war, progressive and independent Great Western. Their impression of powerful potency was accentuated by the fitting of a squat double chimney (in the case of No. 1018 from January 1959). This measure improved the performance which was welcome in the Duchy. The change gave the class a hump-backed appearance but also added an indefinable "something". *RCR7606)*

Opposite top: This view of Truro shed from the south reveals how this establishment nestled cosily into the hillside on a cramped site. On 22 July 1960, five steam locomotives were partly visible but only two can be positively identified: No. 5562 (a long-term Truro resident) and No. 7812 *Erlestoke Manor* (then of Penzance but transferred to Oswestry two months later) standing on the road immediately adjacent to the main line. Two more 4-6-0s are in shot, one standing alongside the Manor and the other behind the pair of tatty departmental vans. An 0-6-0PT Class 94xx is to the right of the coal stage and slightly proud of the shed extension, the driving cab of a brand new diesel multiple unit is just visible. *RCR15193*

Opposite bottom: Truro shed yard on 20 July 1960 looking south with a parade of locomotives standing on the nearer of two storage roads below the main line which curves away uphill towards Penzance. Centre stage is No 6870 *Bodicote Grange* (Penzance) with spark arrester-equipped 0-6-0PT No. 3709 (which had moved from Didcot a few days earlier) to the left. No. 7813 *Freshford Manor* (Truro) is to the right. The spark arrester was required for shunting at Falmouth docks. *RCR15164*

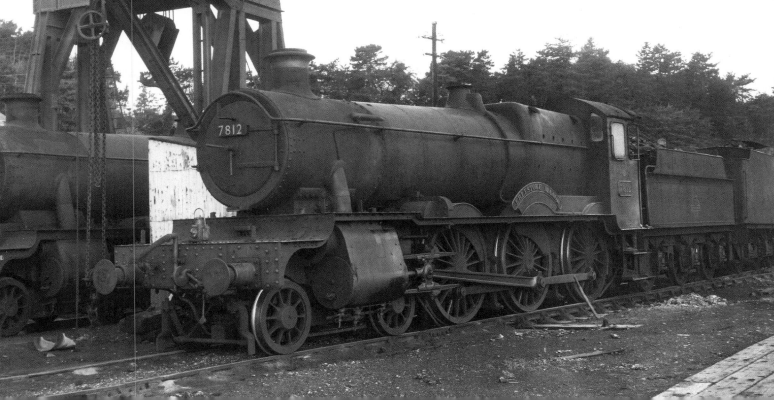

Opposite top: On 14 July 1961, small prairie No. 4565 (a long term resident) and an unidentified 0-6-0PT Class 8750 were parked on the curved siding south of St. Blazey shed and north of the coal stage. The rear of the roundhouse is immediately behind the 2-6-2T and the low-angle gabled extension that accommodated the three longer centre roads is in the left background. The 400 feet long straight siding to the left was served only by the wagon turntable in the foreground. This line ran parallel with the eastern wall of the civil engineers' workshops which are out-of-shot to the left. *RCR16092*

Opposite bottom: 2-8-0T No. 4273 on the turntable from an unusual angle i.e. the inside of St. Blazey shed on 14 July 1961. The key purpose of St. Blazey's 2-8-0Ts was operation of china clay traffic but they did find other work such as empty coaching stock movements (Page 13) and general freight trains (Page 65). Another service was the 10.15 am Launceston-Plymouth SSO which typically comprised six coaches, far more than was probably needed over that branch. However, the working timetable allowed for a pause at Marsh Mills (at the start of the Launceston branch about one mile east of Laira) for change of motive power, a County being the preferred choice from there forward. On arrival at North Road, this train became the 12.05 pm Plymouth-Redruth stopper. The logic was to minimise stock and light engine movements at North Road. From Redruth, the train continued as empty stock to Carn Brea for reversal and return to Truro to form the 4.00 pm stopping service to Plymouth. Laira could be short of motive power on summer Saturdays, and if a 42xx was waiting to return to St. Blazey, it is believed to have been commandeered on more than one occasion to work the Down passenger train to Redruth. Although specific dates have not been traced, this operating pattern illustrates the sort of measures adopted to relieve pressure at busy periods in the West Country. *RCR16089*

Above: This view was taken from the cab of Warship D816 *Eclipse* at the head of a train of empty china clay "hoods" on 22 July 1960, looking northwards from the Fowey/ Par Harbour line with St. Blazey depot behind the camera to the left-hand side. The locomotive is standing at the bracket signal that controlled access to the goods yard on the left and to the Par-Newquay branch. The Par loop curves in from the right to enter the closed station. St. Blazey Signal Box stands at this end of what was once the Down platform. The loop round to Par station was double track and a siding trailed in on the Up line. Originally known as the Ballast Siding, from 1923 this line was adopted for storage of coaching stock to which purpose it was being put on this occasion. *RCR15190*

Above: The Liskeard and Caradon Railway opened in 1844 to convey copper, tin and granite mined and quarried at heights up to around 1200 feet above sea level in the Caradon/ Cheesewring area on the eastern flank of Bodmin moor, to the north of Liskeard. This standard gauge route wound its way uphill to connect with a complex network of industrial lines and tramways that had developed by the late 19th Century. Originally, minerals were brought down to Moorswater by rail and transferred to canal for movement to Looe and onward shipment by sea. Substantial traffic growth led to the canal company opening the parallel Liskeard and Looe Railway (L&LR) in 1860. Moorswater then became an end-on junction between the two railways which continued to work solely as minerals-only systems. In 1862, conduct of the two was vested in a single management committee and in 1879 passenger servces were introduced between Looe and Moorswater.

The system was self-contained and Moorswater station was inconveniently located for Liskeard. Progressive decline in mining and quarrying activities, in the latter part of the 19th Century, made a connection with the national network essential. This was achieved through the Liskeard and Looe Extension Railway which climbed 205 feet from Coombe Junction, 1½ miles south of Moorswater. A terminus platform at right angles to Liskeard's through station was installed which was reached by means of an almost complete circle at a ruling gradient of 1 in 40 through curves with radii as tight as eight chains. The journey between Liskeard and Looe required a change of direction for passenger trains at the Coombe junction passing loop. Freight services reversed further up the line at Moorswater where there were industrial sidings. The GWR worked the two railways from 1909 but with traffic in terminal decline, the section beyond Moorswater was closed entirely in 1917. Track and materials were recovered for use elsewhere. The L&LR was formally absorbed at the Grouping.

Moorswater was another sub-shed that usually housed a pair of small prairies. This two road structure was built by the Liskeard & Looe Railway with workshops housed in adjoining buildings. The line passing to the right of the shed is the remaining stub of the Liskeard and Caradon Railway which was retained as a head shunt. No. 4552 (St. Blazey) on 18 July 1960 had completed the reversal procedure with a short freight train although it is not clear whether at this stage it was bound for Liskeard or Looe. Locomotives always worked over the Extension Railway gradient with smokebox facing uphill to protect the firebox crown. *RCR15099*

Opposite top: Bodmin, sub-shed to St. Blazey, was another ideal modelling subject where, like Helston, the approach saved space by being from the platform road. The allocation was normally a pair of 45xx but none was in residence on 22 July 1960 thus allowing an uninterrupted view of the building and its facilities. The shed provided 85 feet of covered accommodation with a small workshop and office behind; outside stood a classical GWR conical water tower and a covered coal stage. Opened in 1887, closure came in April 1962 although the shed served the preservation community after that. *RCR16086*

Opposite bottom: All but the final two miles of the branch from Plymouth to Launceston were in Devon. On approach to the terminus from the south, the line passed under the Okehampton-Padstow route of the London & South Western's "withered arm" and then turned westward into Launceston. The doubled-up facilities were a classic example of pre-Grouping overkill for the needs of a modestly-sized town. The GWR terminus was close to the LSWR's through station and two locomotive depots were divided separated only by the Southern's metals. Despite the duplication, the two routes were served by a single back-to-back signal box.

The GWR shed, in the background of this picture, was a handsome stone-built affair with 100 feet of covered accommodation and integrated offices. It was opened in 1899 and closed in 1962. On 2 May 1961, light engine No. 5541 (Laira) was passing the shed on foreign metals. *RCR15710*

It was not until 1943 that a rail connection was installed between the two systems at Launceston with the intention of improving operating flexibility in the event of disruption to services in the Plymouth area during the Blitz. From June 1952, the GWR terminus was closed and all traffic used the London & South Western Railway through station. The purpose of the light engine movement depicted in the previous view is now apparent as No. 5541 of Laira has moved on to the ex-LSWR turntable. The GWR depot is in the background and comparison with its counterpart to the south, constructed of flimsy corrugated material and in rather moth-eaten condition, is inevitable. *RCR15711*

Having been turned at the Southern's depot, No. 5541 is now waiting to return over the ex-GWR branch to Plymouth, a distance of about 33 miles. The train comprises a Sunshine series Brake Third and an earlier Collett Composite. In view of the journey length, crews preferred to work the branch chimney-first. *RCR15712*

Chapter 6

People

On an infrequent visit to Britain a few years ago the compiler, anxious to renew his acquaintance with Bristol Temple Meads, politely asked the official at the gate where he could buy a platform ticket. This request met with bafflement and then an admission that the official had once heard of such things from the distant past. Time was when notebook, pencil, bottle of Tizer, ageing pork pie, and a one (old) penny platform ticket was sufficient to guarantee a day's innocent happiness. Now a ticket to travel somewhere is essential, otherwise trains and stations in large part are cordoned off from enthusiasts in the interests of revenue protection, safety concerns, and that great catch-all "security".

A significant portion of Dick Riley's collection was gathered "inside the fence", as was apparent from his activities at the other end of the system. There are enough views of Ranelagh Bridge to suggest that he had the run of the place, and the same seems to have applied at the three main Cornish motive power depots, and by extension the sub-sheds where behaviour would have been even more informal. It would have been impossible to obtain formal permits for every occasion so it should be assumed that his presence was welcomed. Perhaps he was endowed with a persuasive charm that others might envy.

The impression is gained from his work that the line through Cornwall was very much a "family" affair where everyone knew each other, and where there was a strong spirit of co-operation in ensuring the operation of an efficient and important transport system.

--- o O o ---

The brief notes accompanying these two images describe the subject matter as "Foreman Drew and Mr Macy" plus of course No. 4095, on 8 April 1960. *Harlech Castle* had been a resident of Penzance since 1957 but would leave the following month for a brief sojourn at Taunton before moving to Laira. No. 6826 *Nannerth Grange* on the adjacent line was also a local engine, shedded there from December 1949 until July 1962. Close up photographs like this are informative in revealing locomotive detail, and in providing a frustrating reminder to the model builder to include all the ancillary pipework necessary – as the compiler has realised! *RCR14613, 14614*

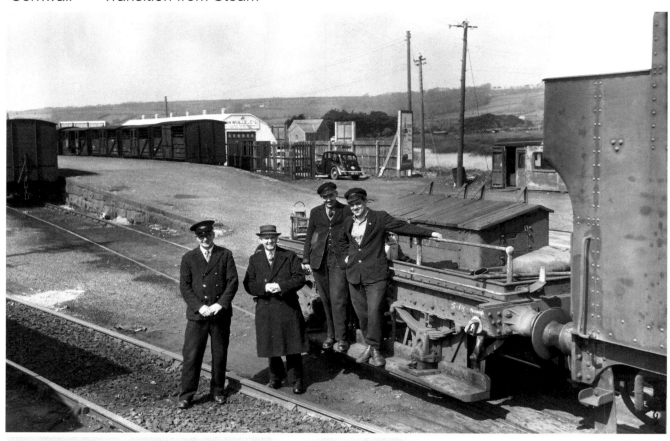

Opposite top: Also on 9 April 1960, Ponsandane was visited and here are the yard staff gathered together beside their shunter's truck or "gig". From other views taken that day, the locomotive can be confirmed as pannier tank No. 9433, a long-term Laira resident that presumably was on loan to Penzance for the broccoli season. Once again, excellent camera work reveals interesting detail. The shunter's truck looks grimy and much used with a variety of odds and ends aboard. The name on the toolbox side is partially obscured and the lettering is worn so the truck's home base cannot be determined; it certainly looks overdue for service and a repaint. In the background can be seen two long rakes of cattle wagons awaiting the next loads of vegetables. At the yard entrance stands what appears to be an aged Wolseley motor car and to the right there is a grounded passenger coach body. Twelve years on from nationalisation and the gentleman to the right has a badge in his lapel that on magnification of the image is revealed to comprise the coats of arms of London and Bristol…..
RCR14621A

Opposite bottom: Again on 9 April 1960, this scene is all of 4 miles on from Ponsandane looking eastwards towards St. Erth station with No. 4083 *Abbotsbury Castle* patiently waiting for the road at the head of another broccoli shipment. It seems that Dick Riley rode aboard the Castle, climbed down and crossed to the Down side to take this photograph. The broccoli train has been side-lined for the passage of at least one train which can be seen in the distance entering St. Erth. The last two vehicles appear to be a Siphon G and a Hawksworth Brake Third. The Riley notes state that No. 4083 is standing with its train in a loop but this does not accord with the Track Layout Diagram for this location which indicates a dead end refuge siding. For the Castle to have moved from the point of departure and then reverse its train into this siding suggests that there must have been a combination of congestion at Ponsandane yard and shortage of paths eastward.

This page: In the next two views, Dick Riley has clearly regained the footplate and, while the train is standing at St. Erth station, has taken the opportunity to photograph Driver Rail looking back down his train while Fireman Harris is on the shovel. *RCR14644, 14645, 14646*

Opposite top: Another example of camera diplomacy with the local gang in company with the last example of the 45xx series of small prairies in its home yard at Truro on 29 April 1961. For such a large group to be able to find the time to assemble for this photograph during a working day stands testimony to Dick Riley's standing among local personnel. *RCR15673*

Opposite bottom: The Counties on their left-hand side looked neat and tidy. The single driving wheel splasher, as borrowed from Castle No 5005 and King No 6014 in their proboscis-led semi-streamlined condition of the late 1930s, gave a sense of modernity. On the other side, the layout was "busier" with a rather makeshift appearance suggesting that the aesthetics had been tackled in a hurry. An independent support carried the nameplate to allow clearance for the reversing rod arm whereas on the other side the plate sat snugly on the splasher. The reinforcing strip added to the valence to support the mounting of the crosshead pump gives the impression of having been an afterthought. The Counties seem to have been built to meet a complex agenda: Hawksworth's determination to make his mark post-war in the limited time available before his retirement; a new locomotive design to complement the GWR's efforts on other fronts toward reconstruction and a fresh beginning; exploitation of new construction methods revealed through experience with other railways' designs during the war; adaptation of the Stanier 8F boiler of which at least 80 had been built at Swindon during the war; perception of the growing need for higher powered mixed traffic engines.

All of these worthy factors were off-set by the design's Achilles heel, the 280 lb/ sq in boiler pressure which was seemingly selected to match that of the Bulleid Pacifics. The pressure gauge was a visible but misleading suggestion to crews that they had charge of a super-Castle while the extra 30 lb/ sq in over that of the Kings yielded a disproportionate increase in boiler maintenance costs. Hawksworth's other 4-6-0 design, the Modified Hall, was an all-round good engine and a more successful application of modern design techniques.

None of this seems to be of much concern to Driver Osborne and Fireman Grainger as they stand proudly beside No. 1002 at St. Blazey shed on 23 September 1960. *RCR15392*

Above: In the mid-1950s, the UK's car population was a fraction of 21st Century levels and while average daily distances travelled per capita were modest by current standards, there was proportionately much greater reliance on public transport. The River Tamar rendered south-eastern Cornwall physically remote from Plymouth and it might be speculated that the lady in this shot is bound for a day's shopping in Devon's major conurbation. The train would have been easily the quickest way of getting there, demonstrating just how important was the railway to the local community in those days. Armed with a large shopping bag, she is intently watching the arrival of the Up express as it coasts into Par behind No. 6931 *Aldborough Hall* (Truro) on 2 September 1954. As so often with Dick Riley's work, his "train in the landscape" approach records so much of the everyday atmosphere of the railway. *RCR5383)*

A wisp of vapour around the steam pipe is the only evidence that No. 7806 *Cockington Manor* was on duty at St. Blazey on 17 July 1960 although the driver's composure suggests that there will be a few moment's delay before work recommences. The fireman, who is out of sight, is perhaps rather busier in the tender. *RCR15090*

The date is 29 April 1961 and the differing ages of those gathered in front of No. 6824 *Ashley Grange* shows the inter-generational nature of footplate crews. Cleaners and young firemen learned the skills and techniques of their chosen occupation while on the job, aided by theory imparted by more experienced colleagues through the system of Mutual Improvement Classes. The two gentlemen on the right, probably nearing the end of their careers, could probably look back with pride over many years on the footplate. The rundown of steam was already well in hand so the three young men would have been aware that modernisation would have significant impact on their career prospects. A little more than two years later, the Beeching Plan would reveal disruption of a greater scale to hopes for the future than those present could have imagined. No 6824 was a Penzance engine for ten years before moving to Laira in August 1962. *RCR15653*

Sixty years ago and a different world. This nostalgic view cogently reminds of how things used to be on relaxed, sunny days thus stirring the richest of memories for GWR enthusiasts of a certain age. Given the casual attire of the audience admiring No. 6800 *Arlington Grange*, 29 April 1961 must have been unseasonably warm, and obviously the pair have been allowed the freedom of Penzance shed yard. It is not clear what the fitter is up to in attending to the safety valve of the admirably clean 4-6-0 but his perch looks precarious. Health & Safety Inspectors look away now. *RCR15661*

Driver Rundle in the cab of D816 *Eclipse* hauling a train of empty clay wagons near Pinnock tunnel bound for St. Blazey on 22 July 1960. Working conditions such as depicted here were a far cry from those that this driver would have experienced at the start of his career. He probably commenced on the footplate as the second man aboard a pannier tank engaged in shunting. *RCR15188*

Chapter 7

Next train

Scotsmen in the South-West? North British-built ROD 2-8-0s and WD 2-8-0s possibly worked into Cornwall under wartime conditions but probably not in the normal pattern of operations. A smattering of Class 57xx 0-6-0PTs from the same builder did reach that far as evidenced by the presence of Truro's strangely-chimneyed No 5744. However, it was only with steam's sad departure that this far corner of England witnessed on a regular basis quite so many locomotives that hailed from Glasgow. Dieselisation west of Bristol was an important priority for British Railways in eliminating the expense of hauling Welsh locomotive coal over considerable distances. The establishment of the new maintenance depot at Plymouth Laira as home for the new fleet formed an important element in this strategy.

The GWR between the wars had at least twice evaluated electrification of the West Country network only to conclude that the return on investment would be inadequate. The excursion into cutting edge technology with gas turbine locomotives had produced mixed results with a major issue concerning uncertain reliability through electrical failures. The dirty environment of the traditional steam locomotive depot was no place in which to service the complex demands of modern sophisticated technology. This experience, coupled with the impressive performances and power-to-weight characteristics of Type V200 locomotives of Deutsche Bundesbahn, argued strongly in favour of the combination of diesel engines and hydraulic transmissions to provide the optimal solution to future motive power demands.

North British Locomotive Company of Glasgow was a significant supplier of first generation diesel-hydraulic locomotives to BR Western Region. The first were the five-strong A1A+A1A Warship Class D6xx (later Class 41) introduced 1958/ 9 and withdrawn *en masse* in December 1967. These were followed by the "baby Warships" Class D63xx (later Class 22) of which 58 were built between 1959 and 1962. They shared the outmoded body construction and external styling of the D600s, and were only marginally longer-lived; withdrawals commenced in 1967 and the class was extinct by 1972. The 33 members of B-B Class 43 built 1960-62 (Nos D833-65) employed a more modern body structure than the other North British classes but were only slightly more reliable. Three were withdrawn in 1969 and all the remainder in 1971.

Swindon-built Class 42 (Nos D800-832/ D866-870) worked for rather longer than the North British version. It was introduced in August 1958 and the last examples worked until late 1972. A notable omission from the black-and-white collection is an example of the stately Class 52 "Western" D1000s.

Dick Riley's final photographic exploration of Cornwall appears to have taken place in 1962 which is understandable in the circumstances. Motor transport was essential to much of his work and it was a long drive from his south London home in pre-motorway days to pursue the slim pickings of surviving Great Western steam. He did take the opportunity to record examples of the new generation of motive power but their modest presence in the collection indicates a magical era had drawn to a close for him, and for so many other devotees.

--- o O o ---

Opposite: Change was evident at Truro on 8 April 1960 as Warship diesel-hydraulic Type 42 No. D813 *Diadem* departed with an Up express, whose two leading coaches were BR Mark 1s. This locomotive had entered service only four months earlier but the 3-car diesel multiple unit standing in the siding to the right is even younger. The vehicle closest to the camera is Driving Motor Second No. W51317 built by Birmingham Carriage & Wagon Co in 1960. It was the first of a batch of fifteen of DMS Nos. W51317-31 which worked with Trailer Composite Nos. W59469-83 and Driving Motor Brake Second Nos W51302-16 (these vehicles later formed part of Class 118). The pristine condition of the engine mounted below the solebar of the DMS suggests that the set is brand new.

The set has been stowed on the siding immediately adjacent to the Down main at the station throat, apparently to enable local personnel to inspect the new arrival. This siding terminated immediately before Carvedras viaduct which crossed Victoria Gardens and when completed as a timber structure was 966 feet long with a maximum height of 86 feet. A masonry replacement was completed in 1902 alongside; five of the original piers still stand in the Gardens in memory of Britain's finest civil engineer. *RCR14605*

Above: Recently-delivered Warships were most readily associated with prestige passenger services so their appearance on mundane duties was unexpected. D816 *Eclipse* had entered service on 17 February 1960 but by 20 July was at work on china clay duties. In this view it was nearing Par Sands with a train of empty hoods, returning from Fowey Docks. Twenty-nine wagons can be seen, emphasising the wider variety of duties that diesel locomotives were expected to undertake in comparison with the steam locomotives they were supplanting. The next day, *Eclipse* could be hauling an express passenger, in replacement of a Castle 4-6-0, but here it is on a duty readily associated with a 2-8-0T Class 42xx. The careers of the diesel hydraulics might have been more crowded and varied but they were significantly shorter. This example was withdrawn on 1 January 1972 whereas in 1960, there were Castles at work in Cornwall that dated back to 1923/4. *RCR15155*

Above: Laira's Warship Class 42 No. D819 *Goliath* was departing from Truro station past the motive power depot on 22 July 1960, bound for Penzance. The Train Reporting Number cannot be reconciled with records for that year. *RCR15192*

Opposite top: Lostwithiel station looking west on 23 September 1960 with a Down passenger train departing in the hands of a pair of D63xx baby Warships. The drab all-maroon BR livery never suited GWR coaches but their heritage remained unmistakable. The first vehicle appears to be a Diagram D121 Brake Third followed by Diagram C77 All Third No W571W and then there is an unidentified Collett bow-ended coach. To the left stands a rake of loaded china clay hoods waiting to be taken down the Fowey branch to the docks. Two bridges crossing the River Fowey are visible in the distance, that on the left carrying the branch. Beside the clay hoods stands a fine example of a standard GWR bracket signal with track indicator diamond affixed. *RCR15173*

Opposite bottom: The North British-built Class D63xx diesel-hydraulics (later Class 22) were an interesting attempt at a flexible form of motive power that could be equally at home working in multiple on express main line services or as single units on branch and local services, coupled to the traditional 2-coach B-set based. Neither idea was long-lived. The concept of double-heading melted away with expansion of the fleet of more powerful diesel-hydraulic locomotives, particularly the D1000 "Westerns". The incursion of branch and suburban diesel multiple units in the 1960s brought premature redundancy for locomotive-hauled non-corridor coaching stock.

On 21 July 1960, D6303 and D6305 were climbing away from Par with a Down passenger service, a scene that would soon disappear with their relegation to secondary duties. Modernisation has yet to affect the train's composition as the first three coaches are a Hawksworth Brake Third (Diagram D133), a flat-ended Collett All Third (Diagram C67), and what appears to be a Collett bow-ender (either an All Third or a Composite). The puddles in the roadway remind that contrary to popular memory, not every summer's day was bathed in unending sunshine. *RCR15167*

Opposite top: St. Dennis Junction was a favourite vantage point for Dick Riley's photographic activities. From there he could monitor china clay traffic associated with the winding freight-only route southwards to the main line at Burngullow, and also Par-Newquay passenger services. The sidings that served the china clay branches that radiated from the St. Dennis-Burngullow route seemed ominously quiet on 21 June 1962 and there is no familiar prairie or pannier fussing about with clay hoods. A foretaste of the streamlined, stripped-down railway that the Beeching bombshell would soon bring about? From another view of this 2-car diesel multiple unit, it seems to comprise a DMS (possibly W51329) leading a DMBS, both built by Birmingham RCW as a 3-vehicle unit, later classified 118. It has to be admitted that the open saloons of first generation DMUs were a welcome change to non-corridor compartment stock. Trailer vehicles were to be preferred as there would be no engine unit rattling away below the floor. The atmosphere inside was light and airy, greatly helped by panoramic views of the passing countryside. In many (but definitely not all) ways the experience was reminiscent of the auto coach of hallowed memory. *RCR16545*

Opposite bottom: Standing in the Up loop just east of Penzance station throat on 9 April 1960 was a rake of modern Travelling Post Office vehicles based on the BR Mark 1 design, a further sign that modernisation had reached the west. However at the far end stands an inside-framed Siphon G, a type that certainly proved to be a survivor. It was a personal pleasure nearly 20 years later to seek out Siphon Gs in the late evenings at Paddington. By then with most of their ventilator slats plated over and daubed in vulgar "rail blue", they were seeing out their careers on newspaper trains, but there was no doubting their proud ancestry. *RCR14619*

Above: Baby Warship No. D6315 was running into Hayle on 18 June 1962 with a Down local passenger train. This class was subject to minor changes during its short career and the first is evident in the end yellow warning panel. It is not possible to determine the nature of the carriage stock but the ventilator lines suggest three different diagrams. This scene is of a railway on the cusp of change although plenty of the old is still *in situ* such as the signals, water column, gas lighting, water tank on stone pedestal, modest station building bedecked with posters and the picturesque signal box. Below the box there is a traditional station platform seat with the cast roundel emblem on the end supports, duly painted brown but with only the "W" picked out in cream. In terms of infrastructure, the new era is so far limited to the motive power, and to the 2- and 3-car stop signs on the platforms.

Yard facilities at Hayle station were quite limited. The string of wagons is standing on the Up goods loop. This served the needs of the Hayle Wharves branch which led to what was once a quite extensive network of freight lines. The branch was approached by a facing junction before the station off the Up line and turned away to the left behind the signal box. The wagons comprise several all-steel mineral wagons plus an old wooden-bodied wagon, all apparently loaded with coal. There are then two or three five-plank wagons and finally a couple of oil tank wagons. Little sign of modernity in that rake. *RCR16520*

Above: On 9 July 1961, D831 *Monarch* was crossing Liskeard viaduct with an Up service. This locomotive had entered traffic on 11 January 1961 and would be withdrawn in early October 1971. This view shows the nature of the modifications necessary with replacement of the viaduct's timber spans with brickwork built on the original stone piers. The walkway installed beneath the steel spans reflects a greater concern for staff safety than was evident in the previous century. The course of the Looe Extension Railway descending towards Coombe Junction can be discerned on the far side of the valley. *RCR16056*

Opposite: Looking back, the early diesel-hydraulic fleet probably deserved more affection than they received on their arrival in the West. They were virtually the last expression of attempted autonomy by the "Great Western" Region of British Railways. At the time they were vilified as the usurpers of Kings, Castles and, in Cornwall, even St. Blazey's Class 42xx 2-8-0Ts. Nevertheless, they were undeniably special to the Western Region, with the B-B Warships proving worthy progenitors to the handsome D1000 "Western" series (later Class 52).

On 19 June 1962, D804 *Avenger* was drawing away from Lostwithiel with the 11.00 am Penzance-Manchester on the Up main. This was a lightweight train of only six vehicles, apparently all BR Mark 1s of which the first is a Full Brake. The all-over maroon carriage livery was dull and depressing in contrast to the earlier "blood and custard" and to the later blue and light grey. D804 does not look much better as it is in dirty, tatty green with its number no longer discernible; this locomotive had entered service on 23 April 1959 and does not seem to have received too much external attention since. Initial operation of first generation diesels was not intensive as they had to work in links scheduled for steam locomotives. As the modern fleet expanded, re-organisation allowed this situation to be redressed and BR seems to be getting its money's worth out of this Warship.

The next line to the right of the train was the Up loop, entry to which was roughly beneath the train's first two vehicles while the next line over was the milk siding that served the creamery, part of the Unigate group. Of the eight 6-wheel tankers standing on the siding, only one appeared to be in anything like clean condition. To the left, two more equally grimy tankers were parked on the siding beside the Down loop. *RCR16532*

Opposite top: On 21 June 1962, Warship D820 *Grenville* (May 1960 to December 1972) was leaving Truro with an Up passenger service. To the left a diesel shunter whose number is unclear is standing beside the smartly-maintained elevated water tank which will not be needed for much longer. The sign on the fence below the tank states "TRURO JUNCTION FOR FALMOUTH". To the far right, a 2-cylinder 4-6-0, No. 6800 *Arlington Grange,* is waiting in the yard with its potato special, as depicted in Chapter 4. *RCR16536*

Opposite bottom: Warship Class 43 No. D840 *Resistance* was approaching Grampound Road on 11 July 1961 with a train of matched BR Mark 1 coaches except for the fourth and fifth which are an ex-GWR catering pair. All those in sight are in chocolate and cream livery. D840's operating life was short, being introduced to service in February 1961 and withdrawn in April 1969. The line on the far side was a long head shunt that was originally part of the single line main line before doubling and realignment of the route in 1897/ 8. *RCR16072*

Above: An Up service worked by a 2-car DMU comprising a pair of double-ended Driving Motor Brake seconds of Class 121 was approaching Truro station on 21 June 1962. This type was favoured for use on Truro-Falmouth local services. Another DMU set was standing in the shed on the left hand road. There were many regrets with the passing of Great Western steam but there was a particular poignancy to the situation depicted. Truro had officially closed to steam in March 1962 but the depot is still intact with all the facilities and paraphernalia of a busy steam shed:- stabling roads; turntable; yard lighting; coal stage; water tank; modern concrete extension to the original shed building; empty ashpit which has been cleaned out for the last time; and in the darker recesses of the complex that wonderful sulphurous, steamy, oily smell would linger on. And not forgetting the ghosts. *RCR16542*

Postcript

An evocative scene that encapsulates the beauty of the Royal Duchy, the brilliant Summer's sun, viaducts and steam. No. 6869 *Resolven Grange* of Laira strides purposefully eastward across Liskeard viaduct on Sunday, 10 July 1955. *RCR6385*